HER NAME IS HEIDI

A Memoir

BONNIE ELDER

Copyright © 2020 Bonnie Elder.

ALL RIGHTS RESERVED. This book contains material protected under International and Federal Copyright Laws and Treaties. Any unauthorized reprint or use of this material is prohibited. No part of this book may be reproduced or transmitted in any form or by any means, electronic or mechanical, including photocopying, recording, or by any information storage and retrieval system without express written permission from the author/publisher.

Scriptures marked NLT are taken from the HOLY BIBLE, NEW LIVING TRANSLATION (NLT): Scriptures taken from the HOLY BIBLE, NEW LIVING TRANSLATION, Copyright© 1996, 2004, 2007 by Tyndale House Foundation. Used by permission of Tyndale House Publishers, Inc., Carol Stream, Illinois 60188. All rights reserved. Used by permission.

Scriptures marked RSV are taken from the REVISED STANDARD VERSION (RSV): Scripture taken from the REVISED STANDARD VERSION, Grand Rapids: Zondervan, 1971.

Scriptures marked TLB are taken from the THE LIVING BIBLE (TLB): Scripture taken from THE LIVING BIBLE copyright© 1971. Used by permission of Tyndale House Publishers, Inc., Carol Stream, Illinois 60188. All rights reserved.

Cover photograph by The Columbus Dispatch

ISBN: 978-1-64184-378-2 (Paperback)
ISBN: 978-1-64184-379-9 (Ebook)

To Heidi and her neighbor Thelma who said,
"That's my girl!"

Contents

Preface ix

1 - Premonition 1
2 - Birthday 3
3 - Coming Home 6
4 - New Doctor 9
5 - Baby Shower or Not? 11
6 - The Qualifying Interview 13
7 - Early Childhood 16
8 - The Healing Service 20
9 - Meditation 22
10 - The Grieving Process 25
11 - Sixth Month Checkup 27
12 - The Sign Post 29
13 - First Surgery 31
14 - First Birthday 35

15	-	The Joys, the Giggles, and the Fun	37
16	-	High Chair Praise	40
17	-	Walking Through It Together	43
18	-	Second Time Around	45
19	-	Red Letter Day	50
20	-	Postoperative Success	52
21	-	Dark Night of the Soul	56
22	-	Lifting Mountains	58
23	-	My Three R's	60
24	-	Broken Dreams	62
25	-	Gravity	64
26	-	Snowflakes	66
27	-	Dr. Mommy/Advocate	68
28	-	Little Sister	71
29	-	Flying Spoons, Dancing Flags, and Other Episodes	73
30	-	A New Kind of Intercession	76
31	-	IQ and Public School	78
32	-	Mom's Growing Up Too	83
33	-	Jumping Hannah, Hide-and-Seek, and Other Bedroom Stories	85
34	-	Social Skills	88
35	-	Class Mother	90
36	-	Camping	92
37	-	Family Church Camp	96
38	-	What Do Others Think?	99
39	-	Tonsillectomy???	101
40	-	Special Olympics	104

41	-	Up North	107
42	-	Dairy Queen Treats	110
43	-	Middle School	113
44	-	Over the Wall	115
45	-	To Come to You	117
46	-	Finding Providers	119
47	-	A Game-Changing Day	123
48	-	Allowances	125
49	-	The Fish Fry and Crashing Parties	127
50	-	My Sister Heidi	130
51	-	Dr. Jekyll and Mr. Hyde	133
52	-	Extended School Years	136
53	-	The Workshop	140
54	-	Technology Girl	142
55	-	Down in the Pit	144
56	-	Heidi's Neighbor	146
57	-	Being a Care Provider	149
58	-	In Her Own Words	152
59	-	To Heidi	154

Acknowledgements 157

Preface

A loud applause exploded from the audience. The singer smiled and then started strumming his guitar again. I settled back in my seat, ready for more great music. When the crowd hushed, he said, "I have a wonderful niece. When I visited her recently, I saw how much she had grown. She talked to me about some of the problems she was having as a teenager, and my heart went out to her. I love her so much. This song is for her."

As he sang, I was touched by the love this man had for his niece. His song was also endearing, and I had a strong sense that it had a special meaning for me. I quickly realized what it was. The name he sang was to be the name of the child I was carrying in my womb—Heidi.

Yes, that was my child's name! I had never even considered this name before. Yet, as I left the concert hall that night, I had a thrill in my heart. Her name was Heidi, and that's how our story begins.

••• 1 •••
Premonition

MY HUSBAND JEFF and I had a wonderful son, Andrew. When he was two years old, I had a miscarriage. After time had healed me from our loss, Jeff and I felt ready for another child, and we conceived again and were very excited. However, since I had lost the last baby, I was feeling a bit anxious, so we decided to pray about a new little one.

What happened during that prayer was unexpected and life-changing. I don't remember what I prayed, but I do remember what Jeff prayed. He told the Lord that it didn't matter if the baby was a boy or girl—whatever God had in mind was okay with him. Then he said, "Whatever kind of child You see fit to give to us is all right." I gasped! That didn't sound so good. I wanted to yell at Jeff to take it back, but I knew I couldn't. It was too late. I was envisioning the prayer already entering the "celestial gears of heaven," and those gears were turning slowly, wisely, and knowingly with that prayer snuggly wrapped in its eternal purposes. While I know that's not how prayers are answered, that is what it felt like to me. Jeff's prayer had been said, heard, and was on its way to being answered.

After that moment and all throughout my pregnancy, I had an unsettled feeling about this baby's arrival. When she was born, I remember thinking this was the kind of thing that happened to *other* people, but not us, right? She certainly was the biggest and most surprising gift I ever opened.

···2···
Birthday

HEIDI WAS DUE on January 26, but she decided to surprise us with an early labor on the 16th. On the way to the hospital we passed a Jolly Pirate Donut shop, and Jeff asked me if I wanted to grab a couple of donuts. We laughed and kept on driving even though I was sure he wished we could have stopped. It was a quick labor, and soon we heard those glorious words: "It's a girl!" Jeff and I beamed at each other. I saw tears of joy in Jeff's eyes as the medical staff laid her on my stomach to cut the cord. She was quiet, limp, and looked exhausted. I had received pain medication, so I just figured it had affected her too. The doctor who examined Heidi left briefly. By the time the nurses had cleaned us up, another doctor came in with my doctor to examine her as well. After this second examination, the nurses left and our doctor sat down next to me.

The earth moved as he said, "We've examined Heidi and feel there is a possibility that she has Down's syndrome. We will need to check her vital organs and run a test to determine if what we think is true or not." We could have heard a pin drop.

He continued to tell us the signs of Down's syndrome: Simeon creases in her hands, almond shaped eyes, poor muscle tone, small ear canals, extra skin on the back of her neck, short fingers, something different about her nose, and more. All of this was swirling around my head as I looked at Heidi and thought how much she looked like Andrew. No, this couldn't be true. It was all a big mistake. They were wrong. They had to be wrong. Please, dear God let them be wrong!

I wondered if Heidi would die soon. I didn't know much about it. However, what came to Jeff's mind was worse. He thought of all the poor souls who were mentally retarded or had Down's syndrome that we'd visited at the County Home. They were so pitiful and forgotten, and they were begging for our attention and love. It was scary. I didn't know it until later, but, when Jeff went to the bathroom, he vomited before coming back to my side.

The doctor talked to us about what to do with her. What to do with her? I was confused because I was planning on taking her home. What else does a mother do but take her baby home? It never even crossed my mind, no matter how badly things went, to do otherwise. He quietly sat there next to me, waiting for a response. I told him that I didn't care what was wrong with her, but we were taking her home and would love her. I told him that God gave her to us, and we'd do our best. Jeff nodded his head in approval, and the doctor smiled at us.

Once I'd moved out of the birthing room and into my own room, Jeff and I were finally left alone with our new little girl. Was she going to live long enough to know that she'd been born? Would she die in a few days? What should we say to our friends and family? Should we say anything or wait until the tests were final? This was supposed to be such a happy day, but now it brought confusion and fear. What did our future hold?

We called our small church and told them the truth. We called our family and said that some tests had to be run because they suspected some medical problems. Heidi was a bit jaundiced, so she was put under special lights in a little room off of the nursery. There was a rocking chair in there that I used when I came to hold her. It felt lonely and not right. I wondered if I would even bring her home. Nursing was also hard for Heidi, and she had a heart murmur. Still, the hospital staff was very supportive in every way.

Whether we were ready to face the big world with our little bundle was unknown, but the time came to go home. Jeff and I did enjoy our candlelight dinner the evening before we left, even though it was a celebration of a different kind. We were certainly celebrating the birth of our daughter, but also, in that celebration, we were both aware of the new and heavy mantles that had been laid upon us—mantles of confusion, sorrow, strength, and joy.

···3···
Coming Home

WE WERE EXCITED about getting home with our new baby and seeing Andrew, but we had to first stop at Children's Hospital to have a blood draw to determine if Heidi had Down's syndrome or not. However, our arrival home was a joyful one, thanks to our son Andrew. Thank God for our little children and their thoughtful ways. I can still remember him coming into the living room when he saw us. He shouted to his grandmother, "Granny, they're here!" He came and threw his arms around Heidi and me. He was so proud of his little sister and wanted to hold her. "Look at my baby sister, Granny!" he said as I smiled through my tears at his rejoicing. When visitors came, we not only had a proud father, but we also had a proud brother. He would say, "Look at my baby sister! Her name is Heidi Michelle!"

My mom's visit after Heidi's birth came to an end too quickly. As I watched her car drive away, I felt the weight of the world come down on my shoulders. I was on my own to care for this weak, little girl who was like no other person I'd known: a stranger, yet my own. She was my own flesh and blood, yet I was afraid of her.

Her Name Is Heidi

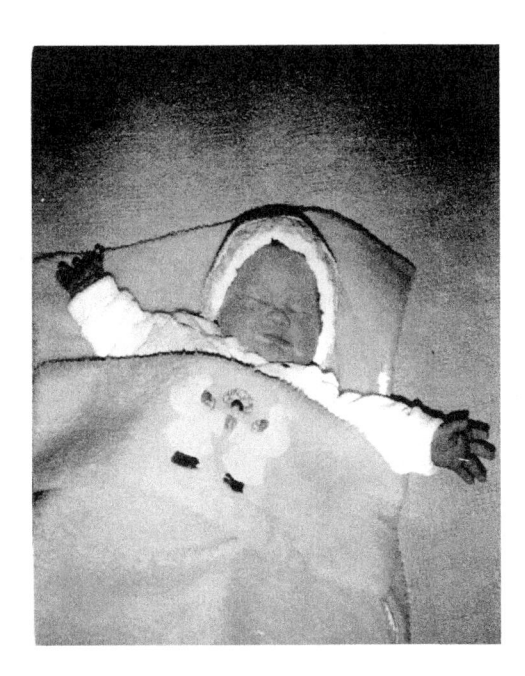

The next day we went to our pastor's home, and he and his wife greeted us. As Debbie took Heidi into her arms, she looked at her face and said, "How precious!" It touched me heart. Then her husband, Joseph, said the most incredulous words:

> Heidi is a love gift from the Lord. You have to face the worst possibility about her, and that is that she has Down's syndrome. It may take you a while to work through your emotions. I don't know how long it will take, but you need to work through them. It's like the stages one goes through when someone near to him dies. First, there's denial and rejection of the reality. Then anger, bitterness, and finally acceptance. You may find yourself at any one of those steps right now. Once you accept the worst and embrace it, God can work redemptively in it for good. He may heal her, or He may not heal her. That is up to Him. He will do whatever glorifies Him the best.

We then held hands around the dining room table and prayed, and an amazing thing happened. As I shut my eyes, I saw the four of us standing, at a distance, before the throne of God. We were standing there praying, just as we were around the dining table, and although I couldn't see God, I knew He was there. All of this happened while Joseph prayed, "Lord, I pray that Jeff and Bonnie will accept Heidi and go through the refining fire, which will burn away all that is not of You. It will perfect their love for You and for each other."

···4···
New Doctor

WE HADN'T YET received the results of Heidi's chromosome test, so we were still hoping against hope. We decided to go to another doctor to see if he would say Heidi didn't have Down's syndrome. We were in denial.

This doctor was an older man, experienced with life and people. He examined Heidi and asked us kindly afterwards if we had come to him, as we had to the other doctors, for a diagnosis about her. We admitted it was true. He smiled kindly and said he believed that she did have Down's syndrome. I don't remember his exact words, but they were soothing and comforting. I knew that he understood our plight and sympathized with us. He told us it was not the end of our lives and we would make it.

It is rather amazing how two different doctors can say the exact same thing, but how much help those words give is all in *how* it is said. Later on, this same doctor was very wise in how he answered all of my questions: When will she walk? Will she walk? When will she talk? Will she talk?

His answers fortified and equipped me for years to come. He simply told us, "I don't know when or if she will walk or talk. I can't answer that question for you any more than I can answer it for your son here about his future development. She will have her own timetable, not the timing of others. When she arrives at an accomplishment, rejoice with her. When she arrives at the next, rejoice again. Follow her lead, and you will be surprised and happier."

What a gift that doctor was to me. I will always be grateful for him. He tore out the old mindset that I held and put in a new one. What he said made sense to us and helped us work through things. In the end, it was not having the answers that helped because he had no answers to give. It was about knowing that it would all come in its own way, one that we could not lead but only follow.

••• 5 •••

Baby Shower or Not?

IN THE DAYS that followed her homecoming, Heidi was not gaining weight but rather losing some. Even though she had started at a healthy 8 lbs. 1 oz., she could not get back to her birth weight. She had to be put on the bottle, instead of nursing, which was easier for her but disappointing for me.

My friends had planned a baby shower, but we didn't know what to do because we thought Heidi might end up back in the hospital or possibly not survive at all! In the face of these complications, my friends decided to go ahead and have the baby shower. My best friend even came from out-of-town, which was a surprise and encouragement.

Everyone at the shower was kind and sweet. They bought Heidi all kinds of beautiful dresses, but I secretly wondered if she would live to wear them. The ladies also each brought a scripture verse, and the one that stood out above them all was Debbie's, taken from Psalm 139:13-17 (NLT):

Thank you for making me so wonderfully complex! Your workmanship is marvelous—how well I know it. You watched me as I was being formed in utter seclusion, as I was woven together in the dark of the womb. You saw me before I was born. Every day of my life was recorded in your book. Every moment was laid out before a single day had passed. How precious are your thoughts about me, O God. They cannot be numbered!

I couldn't believe Debbie wrote *that* verse, and yet I couldn't rejoice in it at all. I still felt that there had been some mistake and it was not wonderful what God had done. Call me whatever you want, but those were my honest thoughts. There was no question of my loving her, for I did. It was accepting Heidi's weakness and disability that hurt to the deepest core of my heart, and nothing helped it. After I opened the presents, we began eating refreshments, and I looked across the room and saw two ladies quietly talking and crying. They were just as concerned as I was—what was going to happen to our Heidi?

···6···
The Qualifying Interview

WHEN HEIDI WAS two months old, I realized I had to make the phone call about her chromosome test. It was a hard phone call to make, but it had to be made. Yes, she did have Down's syndrome. The next step was to find help for her development. Debbie, my pastor's wife, encouraged me to call the infant stimulation program of the county and gave me the number. However, the first time I heard "Franklin County Board of Mental Retardation and Developmental Disabilities," I froze. That name was too big for me! I hung up without saying a word. On another day, I called again and talked to the receptionist. She was kind and asked about Heidi's health and how she was feeding, and we talked for a little bit.

After this initial conversation, a home specialist came to visit us to meet Heidi, and I was nervous about it. Yet the home specialist disarmed me as he lay down on the floor with Heidi and talked to her like an old friend. He was obviously enjoying himself. He was laughing, she was fascinated, and I was immediately put at rest. Finally,

Heidi fell asleep from exhaustion, and he asked us questions to prepare the way to receive their services.

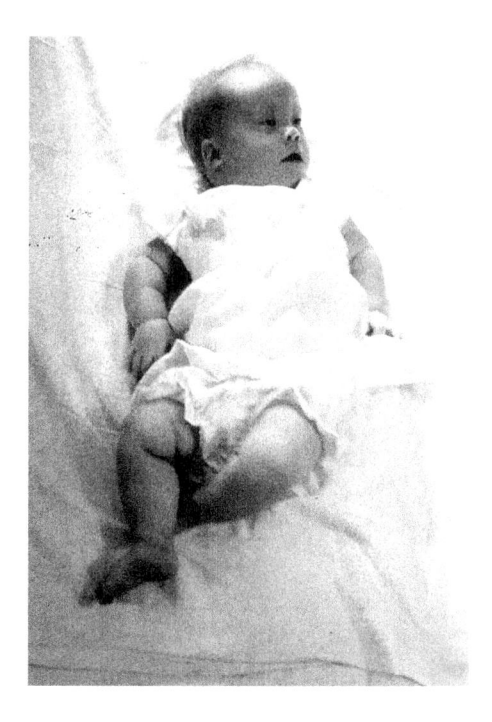

Within weeks we were notified that Heidi would be attending their program. She was three months old by this time. A special meeting was set up for us to meet all of the specialists who would be working with Heidi. One morning Andrew and I set off early with Heidi to visit her new school. It was a small elementary school set in a lovely residential area, and there were glorious flowering trees surrounding us on the sidewalk, which lifted my spirit and seemed to invite us to come in.

Four people were in the classroom: the home-based specialist who had come to our home, the teacher, the assistant teacher, and the physical therapist. I took Heidi out of her car seat, removed her coat, and put her down on the carpet where everyone was seated in a circle. There she was, out in the open for all to observe, and it made me feel naked somehow. When they saw my daughter, would they think less of me?

Once again I was pleasantly surprised as the four adults each held Heidi and talked to her. They each told me what they were looking for and how they would be helping her. Meanwhile Andrew had a fantastic time playing quietly in the corner with the new toys. He thought coming to school with Heidi was a great idea!

When we were finished, the home-based specialist walked me to the door. I felt relieved and received. That day was a real milestone for Heidi and me. We were ready to face the new challenges that school would bring to us.

···7···
Early Childhood

AFTER HEIDI SPENT three months in early intervention, her school took the summer off and moved to a huge facility by the airport. I was shocked and wondered how they'd been contained in a little, neighborhood elementary school only to expand into such a large facility where it was easy to get lost.

There were three "older" girls in Heidi's class. They were all one year older than her, and I was fascinated as they scooted, crawled, and rolled. Heidi couldn't do any of these things yet. In the classroom were shelves filled with toys, which the girls would pull off, and it was quite comical. When the teachers worked with one child, it seemed as though the others would make a disaster of the place. A teacher would (nicely) tell them to stop trashing the room, but they paid no attention whatsoever. On the girls' more ambitious days, the shelf paper even came off along with some of the wall decorations! I could not imagine Heidi ever doing any of these things!

Therapy was one-on-one at first. When Heidi first started early intervention, she was not strong enough to reach out to a toy held in front of her. Still, she would move her lips and try to talk to the toy, which everyone thought was darling. Her teachers held her in semi-sitting positions to strengthen her, even though it exhausted her. In fact, lying on her side with a pillow under her head was even difficult for her. She often cried, and it was hard to watch her go through all the "torture" as it seemed. I often had to hold back tears. There were, of course, those moments of exhilaration when she would finally accomplish a milestone. We would all cheer, and she knew she had the victory.

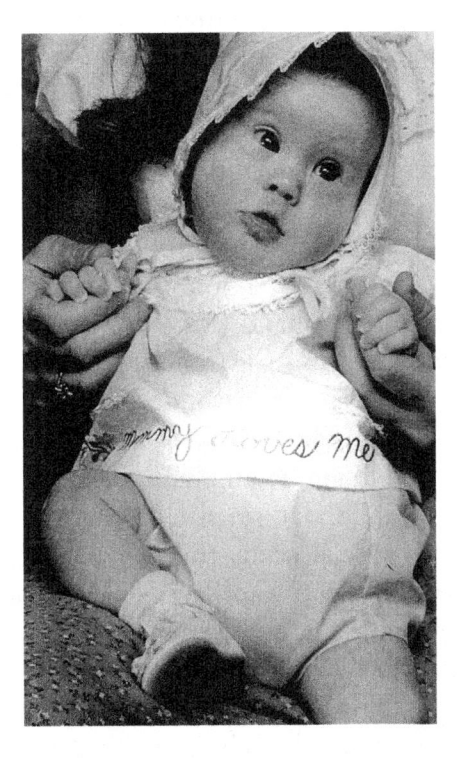

The teachers were young, positive, and funny, and I appreciated all they did for both of us. As Heidi grew older, she eventually worked on the things that the "older" girls had. For example, Down's syndrome children often have very low muscle tone. So, instead of sitting the proper way, they sit doing the splits, which looks very uncomfortable. Putting their legs in a "crisscross" position, like everyone else does, resulted in screaming or crying.

The fun days have to be mentioned too. These days were especially enjoyable for Andrew because he was able to participate and help. A lot of the teaching had to do with the students' discovering textures in the world around them (even though many of them did not like it at all). On one such day, the three older girls were seated at their little round table and had all of their clothes off except their diapers, and I knew something exciting was about to happen. Andrew was placed in command of the activity, and he gave them each a serving of pudding. This, however, was not your usual tea party—the pudding was served *on* the table rather than in bowls, and they were not given any spoons. They were supposed to touch it and hopefully eat it, and, as I watched, the results were highly rewarding. One girl touched it gently and started to cry. One girl happily ate it, and the last one had the best idea of all three. She decided to wear it all over her body. It was in her hair, on her tummy, and on her legs. She was so happy! I believe some of it made it in her mouth. When everyone had finished, the girls were taken to the restroom and washed in one of those round, communal hand sinks. Now that really brought on the screams, both of joy and frustration. Andrew talked about this day for a long time. It was just as wonderful as the day the girls were put in a plastic baby pool filled with Jell-O! The imagination of those teachers never ceased to amaze and humor me.

Part of the early childhood experience was also to help parents in their struggles with special needs children. Therefore, I was invited to attend some parent meetings. I truly did not want to go or leave Heidi, but I went with the other parents. They served coffee and donuts, and then we all introduced ourselves and told something about our child or children. I honestly did not want to tell anybody about my child; I wanted to keep it to myself. It was just too personal for me to share with strangers. However, this was how I met other mothers and fathers who also had handicapped children, and it did bring comfort knowing that I was not alone in my situation.

Many children were much more physically handicapped than Heidi and would remain so for the rest of their lives. One parent had two children in the program! As I listened to some of them talk, I wondered how these women and men dealt with their children's struggles without close family, friends, and especially without God. One mother told us how her own family didn't help with her child who had a serious condition because they were afraid of doing something wrong. It seemed to me that they were just excuses. How alone she felt. How alone she was!

Even though I was still struggling with my own issues, I knew that God had shown up for me time and time again. He always encouraged me and, sometimes, had to correct me, but I knew it was all a part of His love for me. One night when I was feeding Heidi, I was complaining about not getting enough sleep, and then I heard these words: "You have not been grateful or thankful for the gift I have given you." It was true. So I asked God for forgiveness, thanked Him for Heidi, and cried.

Oh, how I wanted to help the other parents! My heart ached with the pain I knew they felt. As I pondered their situations and quietly asked God how I could help them, I heard a voice inside of me say, "Start writing." And that is what I am doing.

···8···
The Healing Service

WHAT IS HOPE? Does it enable us to see what has not yet been? Is it just wishful thinking? Is it thinking aligned with God's truth? All I know is I have to have it, and hope for Heidi was what I needed. Hope for what? I'm not sure. Maybe that she would be healthy? Grow at a normal pace? Hope to have hope? Hope that my pain would go away and this whole dark night would turn into the bright light of day? Hope for a different life?

Whatever it was, hope was the driving force for me to attend a church conference with a prominent pastor in our church. We heard that at the conference the minister was going to have a special time of prayer for children who were sick or had disabilities, and we felt that we should have Heidi prayed for while we were there. I hoped that God would touch her in some way.

The pastor was presented with many handicapped children, including at least one other baby with Down's syndrome, and he prayed for us. He thanked God for our faith and asked God to bless

Heidi and us, parents, too. That was the end. Whatever God had bestowed on Heidi that day was not visible to the human eye.

After he prayed for the children, he spoke to all the parents. "Sometimes we expect instant miracles, and sometimes they happen gradually over time. I suggest that you parents pray each night for your children while they are in the crib. Faith without works is dead, and you need to do this. I believe you will find it to be greatly encouraging to you."

What hope did I receive as I left the conference? It was the understanding that I could do the job God had given me—I could pray for Heidi every night and every day too. Just handing her life over to God made me realize that Someone else was helping to carry my burden. That gave me hope.

Somewhere in the days and nights that followed, God answered a most unusual prayer. I'd been observing other children and older people with Down's syndrome. They all had such large tongues, and it made eating and talking difficult, which greatly concerned me. Out of my inner being came a rather unusual prayer, as I asked God to keep Heidi's tongue small as she was still little then. And I asked Him to keep it that way, even as her body grew larger, so she could talk clearly. I am happy to report that this prayer was miraculously answered—Heidi talks clearly! She also has a surprisingly good vocabulary with which she frequently amazes us. So the incense of prayers rising up from her crib were heard and answered. I give Him the praise.

This plan of mine is not what you would work out, neither are my thoughts the same as yours! For just as the heavens are higher than the earth, so are my ways higher than yours, and my thoughts than yours. (Isaiah 55:8-9 TLB)

···9···
Meditation

WHAT IS MEDITATION? I view it as concentrated thought that's all headed in the same direction. That means our meditations can take us to all kinds of places, right? They can lead us into a wild and stormy sea or into a quiet pasture. I have been to both of those places, and you probably have, too. So, what can help us focus on meditation that is hopeful and helpful?

Here are a few things I've learned. Does saying things out loud help? Yes. Does repetition help? Yes. What else? I've discovered singing helps me focus on words that enable me to see truth. Singing also helps lift depression. It lifts my spirit from down in the dumps to a better place. Sometimes, I've had to sing through tears and choke down the sobs, but I made myself sing the songs anyway. These are a few songs that especially blessed and helped me speak the truth to myself.

Her Name Is Heidi

For thy steadfast love is great above the heavens, thy faithfulness reaches to the clouds. Be exalted, O God, above the heavens! Let thy glory be over all the earth.
(Psalm 108:4-5 RSV)

I will proclaim the name of the Lord; how glorious is our God! He is the Rock; his deeds are perfect. Everything he does is just and fair. He is a faithful God who does no wrong; how just and upright he is!
(Deut. 32:3-4 NLT)

Bless the Lord, O my soul: and all that is within me, bless his holy name! Bless the Lord, O my soul, and forget not his benefits.
(Psalm 103:1-2 RSV)

These songs brought God's perspective to my mind and heart when my feelings were trying to take control. As I proclaimed God's truth about my situation, I found His peace and healing in a powerful way. If I sang and looked up to Him, He came and met me in my sorrow. This process took much time because I was hurt—and sometimes angry—but once the Word of God took hold of my heart, my heart took hold of it.

> *Bend down from the heavens, Lord, and come…Reach down from heaven and rescue me; deliver me from deep waters, from the power of my enemies.*
> *(Psalm 144:5,7 TLB)*

···10···
The Grieving Process

DURING ONE OF the school's weekly parent meetings, a professional woman shared something extremely helpful to me. She had an eleven-year-old girl with Down's syndrome, and this made her an expert in my eyes.

Although I still struggled from time to time with Heidi's slow physical progress, most of the time I was all right with who she was. Nonetheless, I would periodically become upset with Heidi or discouraged for no apparent reason—this woman helped me understand why. She explained that as expectant parents, we all had dreams for our child. Then, when a disabled child was put into our arms, those dreams fell apart. The result? We still had those unspoken expectations and a child who could not meet them.

There is another peculiar problem that occurs with the birth of a handicapped child. While it is hard for both parents, it seems to be especially difficult for fathers. I have two friends who I met at the county program when Heidi was an infant. Sadly, both of their husbands left them after their special needs child was born, and one of the ladies has *two* children with special needs! A psychologist who realized how great the need was for these fathers of special needs children led a program at OSU called "Just for Dads." Where else could these fathers go to *really* be honest about their lives, talk to other men who had the same problem, and get professional help? There was also a sibling group offered, so that they, too, could talk openly with no hard feelings or judgment. I always said a prayer that the Lord would bless that psychologist abundantly. He has since retired, and I hope someone else took the baton to further this critical ministry.

Along my own parenting journey, acceptance and grieving seem to be the two hands that I hold as we travel. Grieving is not bad; it's just a healthy way of facing the truth. However, I think our culture looks down on grieving. Even when there is a death, we expect people to just snap back into life, as though the loss never happened. This is not healthy or real. Admitting that we are grieving is a good thing, and hopefully the ones around us will have the heart to listen without preaching. Even more, I hope they won't just tell us to get over it or say things that hurt and make things worse.

What else has been part of our journey? Heidi has been and is the catalyst for me to learn unconditional love. No performance, conditions, or returns are necessary. And once again, it is hope that helps me day by day to believe that even if there are no changes or improvements tomorrow, we can still make it through one step at a time. Actually, Heidi does give returns every day. She smiles at me and love shines through her eyes saying, "I love you, Mommy and thank you for all you do for me!"

••• 11 •••
Sixth Month Checkup

IT WAS HEIDI'S sixth month checkup, and the routine visit was almost complete when the doctor listened to her heart. She'd had a murmur since birth, but this time she wasn't congested as usual and he was able to hear it really well. The doctor then told me that Heidi was now strong enough to start dealing with her heart problem, and we were to go to Children's Hospital to have the cardiologist check her.

A month later, Heidi, Andrew, and I were in the hospital seeing the cardiologist. They performed an electrocardiogram and an echocardiogram. We watched Heidi's heart pumping on the monitor, and it was rather awesome.

After the doctor studied the test results, he came back into the room. He told me that 50% of Down's syndrome children have heart problems, and 50% of those children have a hole in their heart. Heidi had a hole in her heart! Once again, I was shocked like I was at her birth. *This couldn't be,* I thought as he spoke quietly and kindly. He told me that she would need to have a heart catheterization to determine if she needed surgery.

I learned to not go to such appointments alone after that. At the end of the appointment, I could barely dress Heidi, pick up our things, and drive home. When Jeff arrived home and heard the news, he proclaimed that God was the God of holes in the heart. It sounded so noble, but I wasn't feeling noble. I wished I could respond in such a masculine way, but I didn't. Yes, I knew that God was God over this situation, but I also saw the next hurdle approaching like a huge wall. Would I fare well or not? I was afraid to even begin.

A most unusual thing happened in the midst of this whirlwind of a day. After I returned home, I received a phone call. However, this was not your ordinary phone call. It was a call from God, as far as I was concerned. It was an elder from the church, who never called just to chat, and he asked how I was. I burst into tears and told him that Heidi needed a catheterization and might even need surgery. He responded in the most incredible way. He said that a lot of people go to the Bible and point to the Scriptures about healing and quote them to God (as if He needs to be reminded), but he didn't think that was the way to relate to God. Finally, he said that if Heidi needed a surgery, then we should do what the doctor said. I was both stunned and afraid. I didn't want a surgery because I was afraid of losing her. As it turned out, we did opt for the surgery.

So let us know, let us press on to know the
Lord; his going forth is as certain as the dawn;
he will come to us as the showers, as the
spring rains that water the earth.
(Hosea 6:3 RSV)

···12···
The Sign Post

I find myself in many valleys, Lord,
They almost follow each other.
I hardly remember a mountain in between
Not that it should really matter.

I do remember a breath, a sigh,
A light in my spirit.
And now I see that it was your touch.
Tho I find myself yet deeper.

Help me not to be afraid of valleys
And to be content in each new valley,
For the soil is richest there and when
I come out, oh, how my eyes can see!

Help me to trust You and to see
That as the dark gets darker
You're focusing my eyes, deeper and clearer
And into your purposes, much farther.

Help me to be sensitive to Your voice,
Your touch, your presence near.
You are so good to me, Lord,
You always understand and are
My friend so dear.
          (From "Valleys" by Bonnie Billow)

ONE DAY AFTER school, I was driving on a country road to a friend's home and reading the names of the residences along the way. Some names were on mailboxes while others were on specially made signs. As I neared my destination, a particular sign caught my eye. There, in bold letters, was the name "FEARING." I was so surprised that, as I passed the sign, I looked back to be sure that it did, in fact, say FEARING on the other side. It did.

"You've got to be kidding!" I said aloud, "If that were my last name I'd change it right away!" But then I realized that I, myself, had entertained many fears—even about things that might never happen. Fearing had become just as much a part of me as if it had been *my* last name! And so I told God that I wanted Him to help me and take my fears away.

···13···
First Surgery

HEIDI AND I arrived at the hospital early. There were many forms to fill out, X-rays to be taken, and blood tests to perform. Eventually, I carried her to the Infant Intensive Care Unit and handed her over to a nurse at the door. This ward was for children two years of age and younger, and Heidi was only eleven months old. After I properly washed my hands with disinfectant soap in the steel sink, I put on the disinfected yellow robe over my street clothes and cautiously made my way into the ICU.

This was my first introduction to an infant ICU. As I quietly made my way over to Heidi, I noticed there were machines next to cribs everywhere and beeping TV monitors throughout the large room. Heidi was in a cartoon-covered gown, which was too large for her, but she looked so cute in it and seemed to think this was fun. The rest of the day and evening was spent feeding her, playing with her, and putting her down for the night.

The next day I arrived before the scheduled time of her catheterization, but they had already wheeled her bed into the operating room. By the time I arrived, I could hear her last sleepy cries before she fell asleep. I prayed for her and sat with a friend who'd come to be with me. Before long, the medical staff was wheeling Heidi out, and she looked up at me with a sleepy smile and cooed! She was already awake! One more smile and she was asleep again. The doctors had made it through the test, but the results were alarming. Heidi needed surgery right away because the valve on her heart (Patent Ductus) had not closed at birth as it should have, and the doctor needed to fix this. We had to leave Heidi at the hospital for the weekend to avoid going through the whole entrance process again, and, of course, we visited her as we waited.

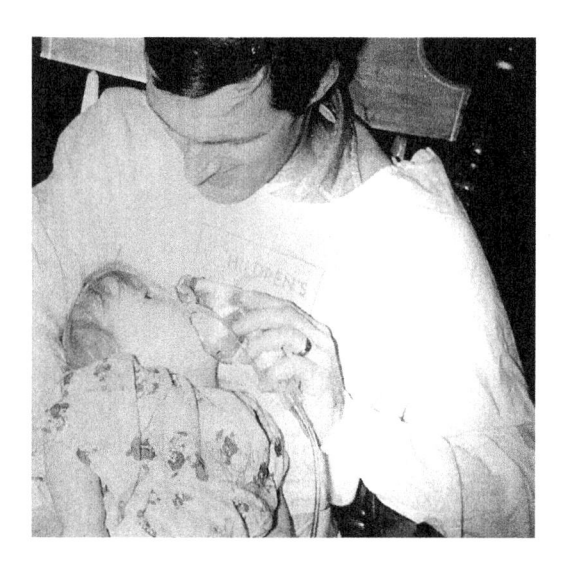

Tuesday came, and Jeff and I took turns holding Heidi before her surgery. We felt awful. We couldn't eat, and she wasn't allowed to. We sat waiting for the medical staff to take her away, and we wondered if we'd see her alive again. A gentleman came to take Heidi, and we walked next to her in her big, metal crib as the man pushed Heidi down one corridor after the next. It was at least a five-minute walk before we had to say good-bye, but she was already asleep. That big, metal crib with its tiny, little bundle was finally pushed through swinging doors. They swung, they shut, and she was gone. We just stood there as a sense of loss swept over us.

Her Name Is Heidi

Jeff and I were the only ones in the large waiting room. We talked and prayed for over two hours, and then we were notified that Heidi was back in her ward. She had survived! We quietly thanked the Lord and returned to the ward to quickly scrub up and put on our lovely yellow sterile gowns.

We were not prepared for how she looked. Heidi was completely naked, and yet we could hardly see her body because of all the bandages, tubes, and tape covering her. The biggest bandage was around her side where the incision was. There was also a tube coming out of her nose, and she had other tubes in her groin, side, and an IV connected to her hand. Additionally, there was a monitor just for her that was beeping and a nurse at her side. The side draining tube made me nauseated, so the nurse brought me a chair. Still, I was glad Heidi was asleep because I knew that when she woke up she would be in a lot of pain.

The next day Heidi could hardly breathe. Her left lung had collapsed, so the only place I could touch her was on the top of her head. When she woke up, she looked so frightened and distressed, and I would stroke her on the head to soothe her. In addition, Heidi was tied down to the bed because otherwise she would have torn out the tubes with all of her moving. Still, it was so hard to see her like that.

One day I asked God how He could watch all of these children go through such things because I knew He loved them all more than I did. This is what I heard in my mind: "Bonnie, you must look beyond the pain to the purpose I have for it." But those words sounded cruel and made me mad.

Once the tube came out of Heidi's nose and she was breathing on her own, there was another ordeal for her to endure. First, the nurse had to administer a medicated mist treatment in a mask over Heidi's nose and mouth, but Heidi was okay with that. Then the nurse cupped her hand and pounded on Heidi's back to loosen the phlegm that Heidi couldn't cough up on her own. I must say that I was startled by the force the nurse used, but, again, Heidi didn't seem to mind that either. But then came the worst part that was not announced to me—her mother! A tube was put down Heidi's throat to suction the phlegm out of her. I was absolutely horrified and couldn't believe what they were doing to her. *That was it!* I thought. I almost slugged the nurse to take Heidi home. It eventually reached the point where I couldn't watch that part of her treatments.

At last Heidi came out of the oxygen tent, but the tube in her throat had been there for two weeks and left her speechless. When she cried, there was no sound. This was the part of her hospital stay that haunted me the most, and it still does if I think about it. It broke my heart that she couldn't be heard in her distress. One day there was a stern, older nurse who didn't seem to care about Heidi's silent cries for help, and it made me wonder how well she was being taken care of. All in all, her first surgery experience had been very traumatic for the both of us.

Finally, the bandages and tubes came off, one by one, and Heidi started to look like a little girl again. It appeared that she was, indeed, going to survive this whole ordeal after all. What a relief to my aching heart. Nineteen days later, Heidi was dismissed from the hospital. She was excited and greeted at home by her big brother who quickly climbed into her playpen to kiss and hug her. She returned the love by blowing bubbles—her special way to show Andrew that she loved him. Our little family was reunited, and all would return to "normal." Thank You, Lord for bringing our daughter home!

···14···
First Birthday

BALLOONS, FOOD, AND party treats were all ready. Heidi had come home from the hospital less than a month before her first birthday, and it was hard to believe that she was one year old already. I was reflecting on the past year of Heidi's life and all that had happened. While it was fun getting things ready for the party, there was still one thing bothering me.

I had invited my friend Debbie to come early, and when she arrived, I told her that this day was bringing a mixture of emotions. I was remembering the struggles, the tears, and the uncertainty we'd faced on the day Heidi was born. I really wanted to be happy, but inside I was sad. So Debbie prayed for me, and this is what she prayed:

> Lord Jesus, we just go back to that day of Heidi's birth. We ask that you go back with us now and help Bonnie picture You there with her through the whole day...We see You there, Lord, as Heidi was born. We see You there, Lord, as the doctors told them about Heidi's condition. We see you there in the days of adjustment that followed.

As Debbie prayed, I saw Him there with me all the way. As my tears fell, the Lord was touching my memories and easing the pain they gave to me, and I saw Him at each of the places Debbie had mentioned: He was there as I cried in my hospital room and as we went home with Heidi for the first time, and He was there with me right then as we were praying.

Jeff had encouraged me to think about the good things the morning of Heidi's party. With Debbie's prayer and God's answer, I had a great day of fun and happiness. I enjoyed my friends, my family, and my daughter. Heidi had fun too.

···15···
The Joys, the Giggles, and the Fun

THIS STORY WOULD be incomplete without adequate description of the humorous and fun-filled events that Heidi brought into our lives. The earliest ones began both early in her life and early in the morning.

It usually started around six a.m. with some happy cooing sounds coming from her crib. If this went on long enough or loudly enough, Andrew would tiptoe into Heidi's room, crawl into her crib quietly, and start talking to and kissing her. Well, needless to say, such affirmation brought on a whole new burst of excited sounds and laughter from both of them. It gave me a smile and a wonderful start to the day.

The floor was another place that brought us great joy because it was where Heidi was equal to us, so she loved having Mom on her back and on the floor. Plus, being on the floor with Heidi made her happy and gave my tired back a much-needed rest. Heidi was a very sociable baby, and when I was down on the ground, she knew her cue and rolled over to me. Then came her happy (and somewhat sad) attempts to crawl on me. She was not strong enough to do this, but it got us laughing. Andrew would help his little sister climb on me, and then Heidi would break out into ecstatic, victorious laughter. She felt she had accomplished a big feat all by herself.

Book reading was already a popular activity with Andrew long before Heidi, so we continued the tradition after she arrived. However, we had to change how we did this. Heidi was not strong enough to sit up, so, once again, we took the reading sessions down to the floor. Heidi would roll over to us and, of course, snuggle up *between* us and listen (well, for the most part she listened). The rest of the time she would make baby sounds—sometimes rather loudly—or reach for the book. It might have been her attempt at reading or possibly her way of saying, "Okay, that's enough. Let's play!"

The next episodes were not meant to be funny, but Heidi has a way of making serious things comical. The setting was the dinner table with Heidi propped up in her foam filled high chair, which was the same height as the table. While this was great for serving her, it was NOT good for table manners. Because of her low muscle tone, Heidi had a way of bending her legs in ways that others couldn't, and at the dinner table, she was at just the right height to put those feet

Her Name Is Heidi

on the table! I know what you're thinking: Well, just move the high chair farther away from the table. While we could have, we didn't always think of that in time, and it was easier to reach her this way. Nonetheless, instead of saying as we do to most children, "Suzie, get your elbows off the table," we would say, "Heidi get your feet off the table." It not only sounded amusing, but it looked funny as well.

Andrew knew that we were trying to teach Heidi proper table manners, so he would not laugh at his sister when he knew he shouldn't despite how funny it looked. But one day I saw something that was even funnier than Heidi's antics. I looked across the table at Andrew, and with a stifled smile on his face, he was slowly sinking on his chair beneath the table. I wondered what he was doing when I realized that he was desperately trying not to smile or laugh at Heidi. He just couldn't keep it in, so he sunk below the table and out of sight. It was a great idea, and I thought he was really a genius. What we weren't counting on was Heidi's response. With a serious face, full of concentration, she watched him slowly disappear under the table, and after he disappeared, she leaned over and half out of her high chair to look for him. Oh, dear! It was too funny, and we all burst out laughing. So much for table etiquette!

···16···
High Chair Praise

SINCE HEIDI WAS old enough to make noises, we could tell when she was trying to sing. We would be playing our instruments or tape player, and she would join in. She joined in rather loudly and joyfully, I might add. She couldn't sing on pitch, so it was an unusual sounding experience. Nonetheless we all continued making a joyful noise, and Heidi's theme song became "Give Thanks." Here are the words:

> Give thanks with a grateful heart,
> Give thanks to the Holy One,
> Give thanks because he's given Jesus Christ our Lord...
> And now, let the weak say, 'I am rich'
> Let the poor say, 'I am strong,'
> because of what the Lord has done for us.

One time, a grown man watched and listened to Heidi sing this song, and it caused him to weep.

Her Name Is Heidi

While Heidi was able to sing, she still wasn't strong enough to sit up in her high chair, so an occupational therapist and a physical therapist came to the home to help with her eating and sitting. Thick foam pieces were wedged in her high chair on each side and behind her. This way she was basically propped up and only had to hold her head up. The therapists also encouraged us to show her some basic sign language until she could talk, and she liked it!

As always, Heidi's weakness didn't stop her from contributing to the humor and inspiration of our family dinner times. The most outstanding experience with Heidi happened when we were at the dinner table and she was sitting in her high chair. Without warning, she started loudly singing, and it was so bold that we were startled. We looked over at her, but she was looking up. In "mid-chew" we silently watched her exuberantly singing to the ceiling. Jeff was frozen with his fork halfway to his opened mouth. I was looking up at the ceiling. Andrew was quietly watching his sister. Then just as quickly as it started, her singing ended. She looked around at all of us, smiled, picked up her food, and started to eat again. Still with fork in midair, Jeff looked sideways at me and said, "Do you get the feeling that we missed something?" I smiled and said, "Yes!"

This happened more than once, and we would be quiet, not wanting to interrupt the Spirit's presence, and I always felt deprived of the visions Heidi was seeing. What a privilege, what an honor, what a joy to witness such pure praise. I have come to call it high chair praise.

··· 17 ···
Walking Through It Together

HEIDI'S SURGERY WAS now almost a year in the past, but it had been a year of constant sickness. It was a blur of pneumonia, croup, and bronchitis, and she had missed a lot of school. The time had come for her yearly checkup, and I didn't want to hear any bad news.

As the checkup approached, I was falling into my fearful mode of operation, but then I came across a scripture that caught my attention: "But thanks be to God, who in Christ always leads us in triumph, and through us spreads the fragrance of the knowledge of Him everywhere" (2 Corinthians 2:14 RSV). That last word started going through my heart over and over again: everywhere...everywhere...*everywhere*! For me, that word meant the hospital, which was my dreaded valley. He was and is and will be THERE! As the reality of this truth soaked down into my spirit, I felt relieved and excited that God had revealed this to me—it was what I needed to fortify myself for the coming days.

In my mind, I saw myself facing that dreaded valley, but I sensed the Lord standing next to me, facing it with me. I almost felt His

Hand on my shoulder while we faced it together. And while the valley was not removed from me, my fears were.

We learned later that Heidi was to have another catheterization, and afterwards we would know what was ahead. There might be another surgery. Still, I knew and know He will be with me as I walk through that dark valley.

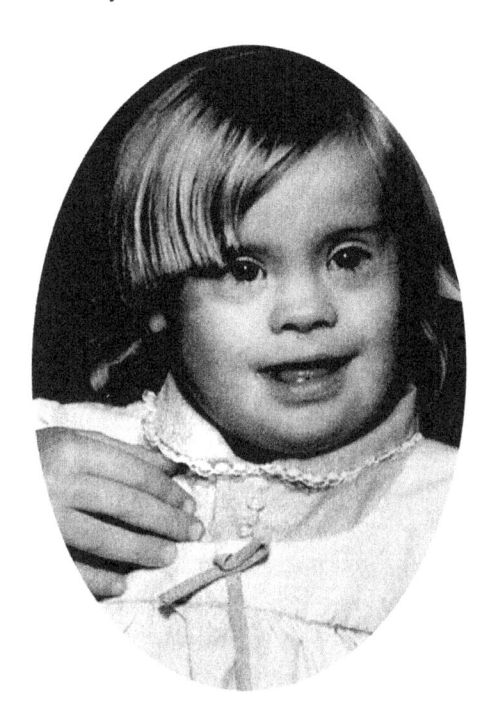

···18···
Second Time Around

THIS IS HOW the doctor explained Heidi's situation. Heidi had a valve in her heart (Ventricular Septal Defect) that needed to be fixed, so he recommended open-heart surgery for her at the age of twenty-two months. Heidi only weighed sixteen pounds, and it had taken her almost two years to double her birth weight. She could grow up with a full life if she had the open-heart surgery. On the other hand, if we didn't have the surgery, she would probably live a year or two and then slowly die from congestive heart failure as her lungs filled up with fluid. *That* did not sound good! While we might lose her in the surgery, we would certainly lose her slowly without it. We were, indeed, between a rock and a hard place! We took the doctor's recommendation.

Knowing God was going to be with me was good news, but I also knew His presence did not guarantee that Heidi would survive the surgery. We had asked a prominent pastor to pray for us before the surgery, and his prayer ended with, "My grace is sufficient for you." To be honest, that ending did not sound good to me, although

I know it was supposed to. I just wanted to hear that she would be okay. Truthfully, I never asked God to tell me what was going to happen because I didn't want to know ahead of time.

The surgery was quickly approaching, and as I was reading Psalm 23, something different came to me. When I read, "Though I walk through the valley of the shadow of death, I will not fear, for You are with me," in my mind I heard, "Yes, Heidi will go through the valley of the shadow of death, but it will only be the SHADOW of death, not death itself. Death will hover over her with its ugly jaws ready to devour her, but death won't be able to take her." I believe it was God speaking to me.

Apparently I received peace after this—at least I appeared peaceful. A friend said he couldn't understand how I could be so calm in the face of this surgery. I replied, "Heidi is as dead to me. Just like Abraham gave up Isaac to God, so I have given Heidi up to God. If He gives her back to me, then I will be blessed." The man started to cry. God had given me His perspective.

When the fateful day came, I went downstairs early in the morning and got down on the floor, face down. All I could pray was, "Lord, have mercy on me. Lord, have mercy on me." I guess it was a pretty selfish prayer, but that was what I prayed and He did have mercy on me.

Jeff and I, along with a friend, went to see Heidi off to her surgery. Again, we walked down the corridors, following her big hospital crib, and watched her go through the same swinging doors. She was gone. And while she was away from us, she wasn't away from God. We found a prayer chapel and started to pray. We expected to be upset, but we weren't. We laughed when our friend said, "This is ridiculous how peaceful we are!" It was true. We even went to get something to eat. Can you imagine that? In the face of life-threatening surgery, we went to eat, and Heidi made it through just fine.

This time Heidi had even more bandages and tubes than her last surgery, if that was even possible. There was a huge bandage right down her entire chest, and her face was covered with tubes and tape. Still, she was alive! I remember thinking to myself, "She's alive; she's alive!" What a miracle it was.

Her Name Is Heidi

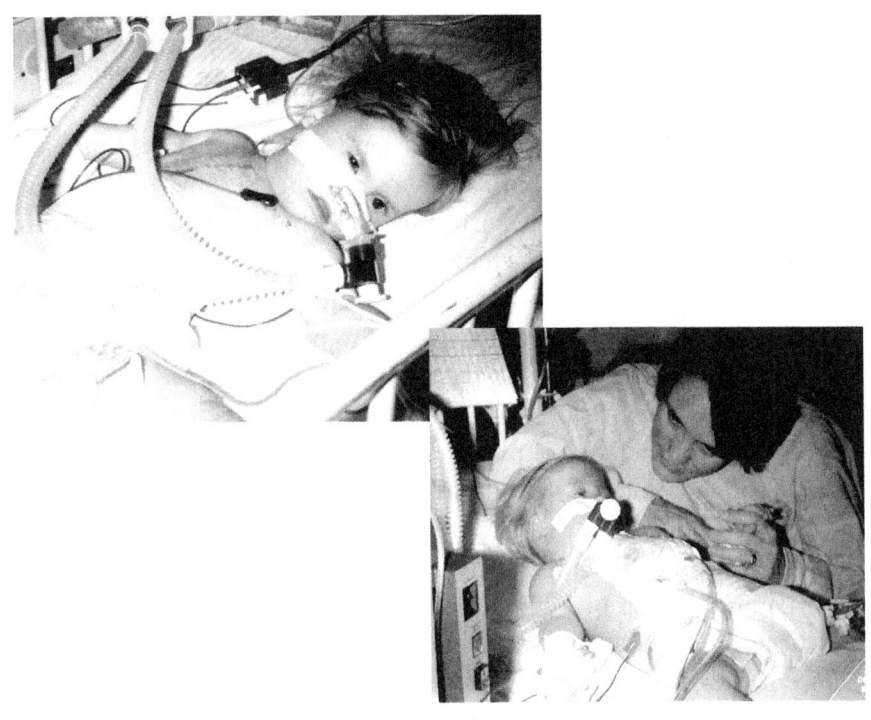

We had just come home from the hospital at 10 p.m. when we immediately got a call saying that Heidi's blood pressure was going down. We quickly called a man from our church, and he said he would call the church to pray. My friend and I put our coats back on and headed back to Heidi. We stayed by her side with the nurse. The nurse was trying to get a needle in to help her blood pressure and tried Heidi's arms, legs, hands, and even her head, but the needles kept popping out. I was holding Heidi down as she struggled against us. It was heart-rending. After too many attempts, I asked if we could get a doctor in to do this, and she finally agreed. Somehow, he managed to get the job done. As we watched, Heidi slowly started to respond, and her blood pressure started to rise. By two a.m., she rose out of the valley of death, riding on the prayers of the saints.

Since Heidi was in the hospital for such a long time (twenty-one days this time), we became a part of the story of the other infants and their parents once more. The head of Heidi's crib was by the window this time, so she had a baby at her right, left, and at her feet. Some babies had extremely complicated surgeries such as making a chamber where there wasn't one. Wow! Others had multiple repairs. Their stories made Heidi's surgery sound so simple, but, as she was weaker than the others, it took her a lot longer to recuperate.

Whenever a baby was in a crisis, the parents were ushered out and the doctors rushed in. It was horrible to watch those parents anxiously waiting to hear the news, and it was often not good news. One mother, upon hearing bad news, ran into the elevator and then raced outside in the snow without a coat. We were all quiet and prayed. In the course of this hospital stay, seven infants died, one day after the next. The tension was palpable as I entered the ICU. The baby on Heidi's right, left, and at the foot of her bed all died and so did three others. Our church prayed for her, and Heidi was protected from the visits from the horrible "death angel." The experience was sobering and sad. After the seventh day, I entered the ICU and saw one of the nurses crying. The nurses were unraveled too; it was too much too often.

One mother whom I'd talked to cried every day when she came to visit her daughter. She really was a mess! She told me through her tears that she used to be a normal person until all of this had happened! We laughed together because I could relate. The church rejoiced that Heidi had been spared, but I also prayed for those parents whose children had died. I prayed that somehow they would find God's comfort and peace, be able to pick up the pieces, and continue somehow through life.

···19···
Red Letter Day

It's homecoming day,
A day so looked forward to,
A day of sunshine and expectation,
A day to finally receive you.

It's your day, honey
You are better and coming home
Lord, why am I afraid to be happy
And still feel all alone?

The time seems rather bittersweet
I can't explain the tears
I want so much for all to be right
It seems like it's been a year...

Her Name Is Heidi

Since you went away just three weeks ago
I cried to God and just wanted to know
That you'd be all right and He'd send you back
Now I rejoice, yet I feel a lack

Of ability to cope with who you are
Though I love you very much.
Dear God, I lean on your adequacy
You are my stay and my trust.

… 20 …

Postoperative Success

HEIDI WAS GETTING better! The tube was finally taken out of her nose and throat after two weeks. Now we saw the semblance of a little girl. She did not like the oxygen tent, but it was better than that horrible tube. And now, finally, she was out of the tent, and we were homeward bound.

When Heidi started feeling better, she was able to express her true feelings about being there, which didn't make it easy for me. With looks that could kill, she said to me, "Why have you left me here in the hospital?" She may have been only twenty-two months old and weighing in at sixteen pounds, but she knew how to throw her little weight around effectively. When I arrived at the hospital, she would give me the cold shoulder. No smile or happy gurgling. She pretty much treated the nurses with the same contempt because they had to do the dirty work, which involved needles. However, if a doctor came in, Heidi smiled. She also flirted with the male respiratory therapist who *was* handsome! He smiled at her thinking she was pretty darling. She knew she was.

Her Name Is Heidi

The infants who survived were released from the hospital rather quickly. One little girl was jumping up and down in her crib just one week after open-heart surgery. I was jealous because I thought we'd never leave. Each day the staff would take Heidi's temperature, and if she had a fever, she could not leave. Another cardiologist really marveled at Heidi and seemed proud of her. She said that Heidi had come through against many odds, and I realized then that the doctor hadn't expected Heidi to survive. Indeed, God saw fit to make Heidi a victor over the odds. Finally twenty-one days later, we were out the door! Yippee! I counted the days and nights between the two surgeries, and it totaled 40 days and 40 nights. We had made it through our own wilderness, and I was grateful.

Once at home the recuperation was very slow. Heidi had to relearn how to sit and feed herself, which took months. It was honestly quite discouraging. Have you ever seen those baby calendars that have stickers to mark a baby's milestones, such as when a baby first sat up, crawled, pulled herself up, stood, and then walked? The only problem with the calendars is they assume those milestones will all happen within the first year. I finally gave up on mine and threw it away. What was the point? Heidi was one to two years behind normal development! Besides, each milestone was etched indelibly in my life—I didn't need a normal calendar for my exceptional daughter!

Still, a disturbing change had come over Heidi after this hospital stay. She cried a lot in the night. I would get up and hold her and comfort her. Eventually she would go back to sleep, but this occurred many times throughout the night and went on for two months. I was exhausted and started sleeping in my pajamas, housecoat, and even slippers! There was no sense in taking any of them off because I was hopping out of bed just after falling asleep.

One day at home church, I told my friends about our nighttime problem. They discerned that a spirit of infirmity had come into Heidi at the hospital, and they prayed for her and told the spirit to leave her. I was holding Heidi when suddenly she reared her head back and screamed, and it was so forceful that I almost dropped her! Afterwards she was quiet and back to normal, and she slept through the night much better after that (and so did I!).

About six months after her surgery, Heidi started to change. Her neck was still weak, which inhibited all other activities, so I decided to sing a song to her to help her along: "He's the glory and the lifter of my head; for Thou, oh Lord, art a shield to me; You're the glory and the lifter of my head." When I sang those words, Heidi would stop whatever she was doing to listen to me and smile; then she'd proceed on with her activity.

Sitting up by herself was Heidi's first landmark. Then she figured out how to get from one place on the floor to the next. Here was her method. While sitting, she would move her crossed legs forward. Next, by leaning forward, she would pick up her little bottom, and that was it—she was moving! When she had attended early childhood, I'd seen the other one-year-olds moving in the same way and thought it was funny. Now Heidi was doing the same thing without anybody showing her how. But her next mode of transportation was something that was uniquely Heidi.

Our home was a large one. The kitchen was in the back, next was the dining room, and then at the front of the house was the living room, which was about twenty-eight feet long. If Heidi was in the kitchen and heard something in the front living room, she had to investigate, so she would lie down on the floor and start rolling. Sounds slow, doesn't it? Not for Heidi. She had that roll perfected, accomplishing record-breaking speed. She would go from the kitchen, through the dining room, and across the whole length of the living room to the stairs in less than a minute. Quite amazing!

Next came the beginner's crawl. On her belly, Heidi squiggled her way across the floor. The therapists told me it was called the G.I. crawl. She was ready for combat, and combating gravity she did. Now she began progressing towards a real crawl, but her head was too heavy to hold up at the same time. So Heidi came up with a very creative solution. She would check out where she wanted to go and put her head down on the carpet. Then she crawled! It was funny, cute, and sad all at the same time. If she bumped into something, she would look again, get around it, and move on. Depending on my mood, I either laughed or cried. This was what I called the five-point, and the therapists thought it was great.

At this point, things started happening quickly. She started to really crawl, and it was only a matter of time until the whole world opened up to her. She was kneeling, pulling herself up into a standing position, and happily climbing up and sliding down the stairs. This was a completely different little girl, and we were excited. Finally she had graduated and started to walk at the age of three years and three months. Her "new" heart was strong, and she received the power and energy she'd been wanting for a very long time. From then on, the house was hers.

···21···
Dark Night of the Soul

THE DARKNESS IN my soul lasted for two years. I just couldn't seem to shake myself out of it. I received prayer weekly, but darkness remained. This is how I felt:

> *He has brought me into deepest darkness, shutting out all light. He has turned against me. Day and night his hand is heavy on me...He buried me in dark places, like those long dead. He has walled me in; I cannot escape...He has filled me with bitterness and given me a cup of deepest sorrows to drink. (Lamentations 3:2-3, 6-7, 15 TLB)*

Part of my problem was I believed a lie—I thought God had betrayed me. The beginning of a breakthrough started with a card I received with the following verse on the front: "I will never leave you or forsake you." As I pondered those words, I heard the Lord ask me a question, which started a conversation between us.

The Lord: "Do you believe that I WILL never forsake you?"

Bonnie: "Yes, Lord. I believe that in the future you WILL never forsake me."

The Lord: "Do you believe that I won't forsake you NOW?"

Bonnie: "Yes, Lord, I believe that you won't forsake me NOW in the present."

The Lord: "Do you believe that I didn't leave you or forsake you in the PAST?"

I couldn't answer because I had started to cry.

As I cried, He spoke more: "You felt like I forsook you. You felt like your friends forsook you. But I didn't forsake you, and they didn't. It has all happened according to My Plan and Purposes. Do you believe this, Bonnie?"

"Yes, Lord," I wailed.

My tears of despair turned into ones of gratitude when I realized that I hadn't been forsaken. God didn't even have the capacity to forsake me—I was His!

> *When you put a seed into the ground it doesn't grow into a plant unless it "dies" first. And when the green shoot comes up out of the seed, it is very different from the seed you first planted. For all you put into the ground is a dry little seed of wheat or whatever you are planting, then God gives it a beautiful new body—just the kind He wants it to have. (1 Corinthians 15:36-38 TLB)*

I was truly hoping that I would come out on the other side of this whole experience a different person than when it all began.

···22···
Lifting Mountains

HEIDI HAD SURVIVED both surgeries, and so had I. She was now two years old, but I was still carrying a deep sorrow about Heidi that I couldn't shake. I could have good days, yes, but deep underneath, my sorrow remained like a stone in my heart. I kept asking for prayer after church each Sunday, and Debbie would pray for me.

One Sunday during Heidi's second year, I went up front *again* for prayer. Debbie came over faithfully to me and put her hand on my shoulder. I heard her sigh deeply and then say, "Lord, only You know how Bonnie feels seeing her daughter the way she is…." Silence. Then something exploded inside me; I almost heard it! I realized that the Lord had been with me all along, and I mean *really* with me! He KNEW how I felt. He felt it too because Heidi was His creation, His beloved girl. He made her, designed her, and loved her. Knowing that He understood me and my pain freed me.

The Lord's fellowship in my suffering was good enough for me, and the chains of deep sorrow fell off. I knew I was going to be okay because someone DID understand. Someone DID know how I felt,

Her Name Is Heidi

and I needed that. Someone was in it with me—I was not alone. Even more, I was in good company, and it changed everything.

I felt hope settle into my spirit. I was free, and I smiled. I knew I was different. And yes, there are difficult days and discouraging times; however, there is never that deep sorrow. It is gone. I am grateful for Debbie's patience and God's faithfulness in answering my deepest prayers.

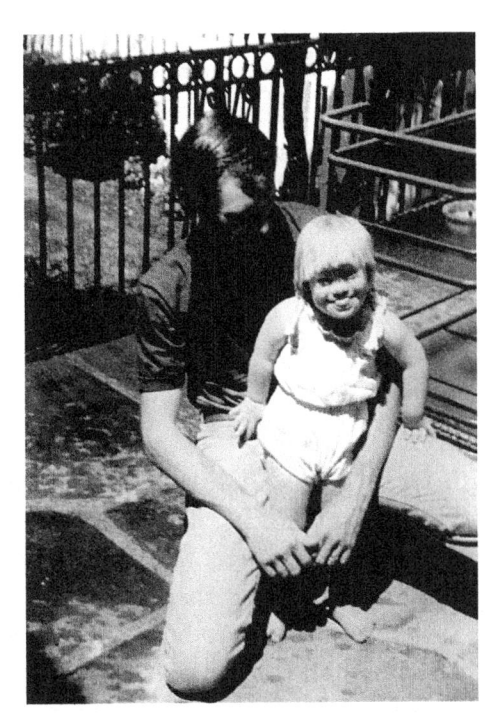

···23···
My Three R's

AS MY LIFE with Heidi unfolded, it became apparent in many situations that I had to advocate for her alone. Sometimes my husband was working and couldn't be there for important appointments. Sometimes he just couldn't handle the burden of those decisions, which made me feel very lonely. My husband was very good with Heidi as an infant, young child, and now as an adult. He has always enjoyed her and loves her. So, in that regard, I was blessed. But most moms have to fend for themselves, which is why I recommend finding a support group and connecting with a new friend there. It helps to talk things through and get the support you need.

I'll never forget a particular parent meeting at school. I had picked up a cup of coffee and a donut from the back of the room and made my way to a seat. I wondered what the topic of discussion would be this time. As I started to listen, I realized the speaker was a woman from the mental health center in town. "Boy, I know that we have problems here, but I didn't think they were *that* bad," I thought and chuckled to myself.

Her Name Is Heidi

Her simple outline was one that I could easily memorize and hopefully put into action: Recognize...Reconstruct...Rest. Recognizing when I was overstressed wasn't too hard, but reconstructing was more difficult. One can't reconstruct unless there are other sources to help, and sometimes there is no one else to help, which is just awful. I did ask friends when I was really low, and sometimes they could help. However, the best thing I *could* do was to eliminate every extra and unnecessary thing from my schedule. That was within my power, and it did help at times. I learned to say no to requests or opportunities that presented themselves to me, and I am still learning that skill.

The last part of the plan was the hardest part for me—rest. The only ways I knew how to do this were to sit with my feet propped up, drink something slowly, and read or do nothing for a half hour or so. It did help, and after a few weeks, I felt revived and ready to return to those extra things that I'd dropped temporarily.

Lift up your heads...and be lifted up...
that the King of glory may come in!
(Psalm 24:9 RSV)

···24···
Broken Dreams

He's the restorer of broken dreams
He gives us a brand new start
He holds the sorrows of us all
And cares for the broken heart.

And so important, to Him, I see
Is when we go right on
Reaching out our hands to Him,
And in our heart singing His song.

For we can each see in our lives,
As the unexpected happens,
He is forming deep within us
Something that will later, gladden...

Her Name Is Heidi

Our present broken heart and soul
Our present unanswered prayers
He is teaching us that He sees all
He is molding our souls so bare.

We need not fear the fears and trials
We need not fear the tears
We need not fear what He may do to us
The Restorer of our years.

We need not fear ourselves
We need not fear any strife
For He is here with us always
The Restorer of our life.

So as the Lord has dealt with us
And dealt down deep within,
The love and patience that becomes our own
Is a gift to us from Him.

···25···
Gravity

WHAT CHILD DOESN'T like watching gravity take an object from his or her hand and send it to the floor? If we really stop to think about it, it is rather fascinating. Well, Heidi was no exception to this childhood wonder.

After breakfast, our morning routine usually involved going upstairs to make beds and collect laundry. I had to be sure Heidi didn't take the fast lane down the stairs, so I put up a gate at the top of the steps. After a half hour, when I was ready to go downstairs, I would remove the gate, and this is when I'd see all of the toys and other items Heidi had slipped through the gate. She had happily watched them bounce down the steps and out of sight, and there before us was a beautiful collection of her prized possessions on the landing. We would giggle while picking them up and know that the next morning it would happen all over again. Heidi was very happy with her morning accomplishment, and her mind was experimenting in its own way.

When Heidi grew older and spent a lot of time outside, she discovered ants. She grabbed a magnifying glass on her own and lay down on the sidewalk to study the little insects. She would do this for hours. Thankfully, Heidi didn't cook the ants in the sun for which I am glad, but she did enjoy her own science class in the backyard.

One other outdoor activity that was truly her favorite was blowing bubbles. She would sit down between our house and the neighbor's and go to it. When I was working in the kitchen, I would see bubbles drifting to the sky, and it was enjoyably quiet and peaceful. Heidi was making the world a prettier place in her own special way.

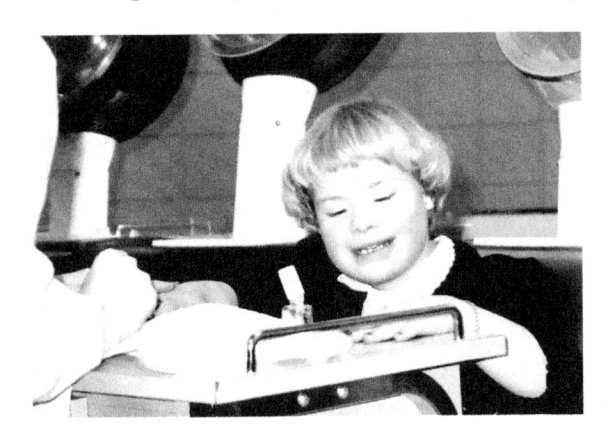

Others also noticed Heidi's contributions to the world. Once a man from church wrote our family a letter after spending time with us. Our Heidi had made quite an impact on him, which he revealed when he wrote the following:

> Heidi faces *and overcomes* more challenges in an hour than most of us do in a week. When we first see Heidi, many of us wish we could reach out and somehow make her "better." But when we look closer and see her courage, determination, and perseverance we become aware that it is she who can make us better.

True words, indeed!

···26···
Snowflakes

I LOVE THE snow and being outside in the winter. I love the fresh air swirling around me. It probably comes from all of my years of skiing as a youngster. However, life was different for Heidi. She could not be in the wind at all, even if it was sixty degrees outside, or else she would get sick. In order to eliminate this problem, we just put a blanket over her head everywhere we went, even in the spring and fall, and we became used to protecting her in this way.

When Heidi was four years old, I went to get Andrew from down the street, so I wrapped Heidi up in a snowsuit and blankets, put her on a sled, and headed out the back gate. She had been feeling well that winter, and I was feeling brave so I didn't cover her head. We ventured out in the cold air like two birds flying out of their cages. I breathed in the cold air and could picture myself out on a ski slope once again. As we rounded the corner, I turned around to see how Heidi was doing, and what I saw was worth recording in my journal.

There was the most unusual expression on her face. It was one of wonder and surprise. Plus, she was shaking her head in little jerking motions and blinking her eyes—I realized it was her first encounter with snowflakes! They were landing on her eyes and nose! She looked so thrilled that tears filled my eyes. After four years, the beauty of this discovery was glowing on her face and in my heart. The outdoors mom was finally able to introduce her indoor daughter to the winter wonderland, and she loved it.

···27···
Dr. Mommy/Advocate

AS AN INFANT, Heidi often struggled with breathing. If she got up to 55 breaths a minute, I was to take her to the ER, and this was frightening. She got close to 55 one night, so I called two of the church elders who lived nearby to come and pray for her. They came right away. They first prayed for her; then they prayed for me.

Heidi's bedroom had turned into a miniature hospital room. We came up with a way to help her breathing by elevating one end of her crib mattress. Next we covered her crib with a sheet and aimed the vaporizer under the sheet. She had her own little sauna! However, there was a problem with this system. The next morning, we would find Heidi all the way down at the bottom of the crib and curled up in a little ball. There was one other problem as well. We lived in an old home that was built with plaster walls and ceilings, and our nightly moisture treatments were taking its toll—a large part of the plaster ceiling was coming loose. We replaced the section with dry wall, and all was well after that. That was a LOT of vaporizing!

Her Name Is Heidi

Along with tracking her breathing, I also had to call the doctor every time Heidi was "wheezing." The nurse would ask all kinds of questions, and I had to learn how to intelligently answer them. I decided it was time to get my own stethoscope. As I was buying it, the lady at the pharmacy looked at me and said, "Oh, Lord, now she has a stethoscope!" I told her, "How else will I know what to say to the doctors?" I soon learned the trick of listening to Heidi's chest. While my descriptions were not medical, they were very understandable—even to a doctor. Her chest either sounded like a sick cow lowing, the snapping-crackling-and-popping sound made when crunching up paper, or just plain ol' wheezing. In the end, we all communicated well with each other. One day, that ornery pharmacist saw me in line at the store, and even though I was clear at the end of the line, she called out to me, "Hey, Dr. Billow! How ya doin'?" Everybody in the line turned around to see to whom she was talking. I smiled and said, "Just fine!" That will teach me to buy a stethoscope!

Speaking of my amazing listening skills, they actually came in handy once in the ER. Heidi was very sick and couldn't eat or drink, but the doctors couldn't seem to figure out what was wrong. Two doctors listened to her and said they didn't hear anything strange, but I told them I'd heard a problem in the upper left side of her lungs. They couldn't give Heidi any medicine because she vomited it up, so we were at a stand still. However, I told them that I wasn't going to leave until they did an X-ray to see if she had pneumonia.

Well, we had the X-ray taken, and I am sure you can guess what they found. Nobody ever apologized, but the receptionist told me with his head down and looking at the papers on his desk that... Heidi had pneumonia...in the upper left side of her lungs. Then he looked up and smiled a very discrete smile. Why can't doctors listen to parents? It was a wonderful thing for me to have a stethoscope. It could put me at ease in the middle of the night if Heidi was having trouble breathing, and it also helped me to answer questions over the phone when necessary.

Heidi had her own relationship with her doctors, too. When we were in another heart doctor's office, she was still in diapers and sitting on the floor. Before the doctor entered the room, I told Heidi to say hi to *Doctor* Craenen, not just Craenen. In comes the doctor and she immediately sits on the floor next to Heidi. Out of Heidi's mouth comes, "HI CREANAN!" The doctor smiled at her and said, "I love these mongoloid children!" Yes, she was an older doctor and apparently hadn't noticed that the label had changed in the last fifty years! Still, we loved her.

Well, in the end, all of the doctor's visits and heart surgeries really paid off because during Heidi's seventh year she made it through the spring AND fall without getting sick! I felt as though God was giving us a diploma. In fact, she was not sick that entire year, and it made a big impression on me. Even though there was a lot of sickness going around that year with children, Heidi did not catch any of it. It was our turn to be healthy, and what a nice break that was!

···28···
Little Sister

I REMEMBER GOING to a parents' group at Children's Hospital during one of Heidi's stays. It was called Patches, and there was only one couple and myself, along with the professional counselor. The couple had just lost their only child to a heart surgery and didn't know whether or not to have another child, so they asked the counselor what he thought. His answer was excellent. He said that you know you are ready to have another child if your desire for one is greater than your fear of having another child with a disability or heart problem. When the time came, I was not afraid of having another child even if he or she had Down's syndrome.

When Heidi was almost four, we received another little girl, Deborah, into our family, and it was a very good thing for Heidi. She had her older, protective brother who talked to her all the time, and then she got to be the big sister for a while. Heidi was fascinated with this little thing who couldn't crawl or talk, and she loved Deborah and kissed her. As Deborah grew older, the girls played dolls and enjoyed lots of little girl things together. It was fun watching them play together.

Ever since Heidi was born and I saw how much Andrew loved her, I decided not to say anything about her disability. I didn't want to ruin the beautiful relationship between them. When he asked why I was crying when she was still an infant, I told him that she was sick, and she was! I figured that if he had questions then he would ask them, so I never said anything about Heidi's mind or development. I also never said anything to Deborah. They both just figured it out in their own minds and accepted Heidi as she was. Now that they are all adults, I've asked them if they agreed with how it all unfolded. Deborah definitely agreed, and Andrew said yes, too. They were glad I let them make their own discoveries.

···29···
Flying Spoons, Dancing Flags, and Other Episodes

WHEN THE GIRLS were still young, we had an old station wagon that was a rather interesting vehicle. Behind the front seat, panels could be rearranged to make a flat bed or a seat facing backwards. This seat is where this story takes place.

Heidi loved toys that rattled, so I let her play with my kitchen spoons. I had a couple of sets, so I gave Heidi her own to enjoy. On this particular day, she decided to bring her spoons on our car ride. As you may guess, the scientist in her mind took over, and Heidi decided to play with gravity and moving air and suddenly out went the spoons! Deborah let out a shout, and I quickly pulled over to the side of the road to retrieve the spoons while avoiding oncoming traffic.

I hate to admit it, but we were all laughing. As we merrily went on our way, the little flags that the girls danced with also flew out of the window! Once again, I pulled over and risked my life to bring those flags back to the car. Needless to say, we finally had to close the back window, but what a shame—it was such a lovely day.

Another episode happened with my mother. We were out shopping and not paying close enough attention to Heidi when, all of a sudden, we couldn't find her. We were in a large department store, and I started to panic. We called out for Heidi, but there was no answer. Finally we spotted her. She was happily riding up the escalator—all by herself! I called out to her again, and she saw me and smiled. I ran to catch up to her while my mom stayed at the bottom of the "down" ride in case I missed her, which I did. Between the two of us, we managed to retrieve Heidi and share a collective sigh of relief. Despite the chaos, Heidi was very happy, and we were very happy to go home.

Our final episode involves a restaurant. Have you ever noticed the mess some people leave after dining out with small children? I have and think it is extremely inconsiderate. Well, I am here to tell

Her Name Is Heidi

you that I was such a mother on one unsuspecting day. We were at a Wendy's restaurant when it occurred. Heidi sat next to me, and Deborah sat next to Andrew in our booth. As we got up to leave, I watched Heidi slide off our bench, and left in her place were so many piles of breadcrumbs that I was in awe as to how that could be! I just stared at them with my mouth hanging open.

I would have been okay and just cleaned up the mess, but Andrew's humor did me in. He said, "Mom, there are more crumbs on that seat than there were in her sandwich!" I burst out laughing and couldn't stop. Then the laughter led to loud hysteria. I knew people were watching me, which made it even funnier because I couldn't do a thing about it. I realized I was out of control, so, while crying blinding tears, I grabbed my purse and Heidi's hand, and we ran out of the restaurant still laughing while Andrew trailed behind with Deborah.

Entering the safe harbor of our car, I gasped for air until I finally stopped laughing. I thought about the mess we'd left behind and felt badly about it, but I was too embarrassed to go back and clean it up. I was one of *those* messy restaurant mothers and couldn't do a thing about it.

···30···
A New Kind of Intercession

WHEN I THINK about who is an intercessor, what comes to mind is a mature, experienced person who has spent a lot of time in God's presence. I have come to see that this is not always the case.

Heidi is as at ease in the presence of God as she is while breathing. She does not feel inadequate or as though she has to do something to deserve His love. She just knows God loves her, and she loves Him.

The way Heidi goes to sleep is through singing, and she puts the names of her friends in the songs she sings. When she started making this a nightly ritual, I became aware that Heidi was praying for these friends. She would say their names and then keep on singing. I realized that this was a very effective way of praying for others: Lift them up to God and then let Him minister to their needs while continuing to worship.

In our big, old brick home where we raised our children, we had a large fireplace, and we loved making a big fire in it and roasting marshmallows. On cold winter nights, the kids would bring their sleeping bags downstairs and enjoy the soft glow of the fire with all

Her Name Is Heidi

the lights off. After the marshmallows were eaten, they would snuggle into their sleeping bags, fluff up their pillows, and go happily to sleep. One time Heidi told a friend that when she went to Heaven she wanted to roast marshmallows in a fireplace with Jesus. What a picture of fellowship. How simple and how sweet! As I live with Heidi, I watch, listen, and learn. I see simplicity, purity, and power. I hope that someday I will catch up to her in these qualities.

···31···
IQ and Public School

ONE OF THE biggest concerns I'd had since Heidi was born was public school. Oh dear, where would she fit in there? As long as Heidi was at the county program, I was assured that she was treated well and understood by all staff members, but public school was going to be completely different. There might be cruel kids and maybe even some cruel teachers.

Like it or not, when Heidi turned six, she was set up to be evaluated by a public school psychologist. Her assessment would determine where she was going to be placed. I remember being nervous about the psychologist coming to my home to share the test results because I didn't want to hear how low Heidi's IQ was. For some reason, it really bothered me, so I prayed before the woman came and hoped I wouldn't fall apart when she told me how low Heidi had scored.

A very interesting thing happened at our meeting. The psychologist told me a lot of things about Heidi, and when she came to Heidi's overall IQ, I held my breath. Heidi's score was, indeed, very low, and it was not in the mildly delayed but the *moderately* delayed category. I was absolutely stunned that her score was so low. I mused about how well Heidi talked and understood things and how good her vocabulary was. Then a wonderful thought came into my mind: "See what great things I have done for her?" I realized that with such a low IQ, it was rather miraculous that Heidi was functioning at a much higher level than what one would expect. In fact, I was told that she was too "high functioning" to remain in the county program, and she would have to go to a regular public school and be in a special class.

Heidi was placed in a resource room, which meant that she had her basic subjects taught to her there. Then she was "mainstreamed" with her non-disabled peers for lunch, recess, some library activities, and assemblies. Later on, it would include art, music, gym, and even home economics. Her first teacher was a wonderful young woman who really worked hard to help Heidi learn her functional words. These were everyday words such as, ladies' room, men's room, exit, enter, danger, do not enter, wet floor, stop, and so on. When Heidi grew older, she knew 180 functional words and was proud of it (and I was proud of her).

Still, I had other concerns and talked to her teacher about them. The first one concerned how Heidi got along with the other children in her other classes. The teacher said that Heidi had a kind of "following" of kids who just loved her. For instance, once there was a picnic, and Heidi was well taken care of by a boy who brought her a plate full of food! She simply sat there and let him serve her as she gave him a big smile. Actually, Heidi still takes on this mode of waiting to see if someone will make the effort to serve her. I smiled; I should have known. Heidi was such a sociable kid. Maybe she would make it in this big bad world after all! Another concern I had was transportation, but it was not Heidi's. She *loved* riding the bus ever since four years of age. Regardless, I hated sending my "baby" on that big yellow bus, even though she wore a harness so she wouldn't fall off her seat.

Her Name Is Heidi

While there were many positives, there were also some very serious issues with attending public school. Heidi was in classes that were originally called Transitional Developmental Handicapped. These classes were mostly made up of other kids who were mentally challenged but were basically behaviorally acceptable in most situations. However, every year or so, we had some children who should have been placed in more restricted rooms or behavior rooms. When Heidi came home saying words I knew she'd never heard at home or told me, "Someone hit me," I would go and investigate. Sometimes it was hard to control some of these students, and, while the teachers apologized, they couldn't place those children in a more adequate setting because the parents would not sign for a change of placement.

There was another situation when the teachers didn't make any attempt to work with students on letter recognition or learn what sounds the letters made. As a matter of fact, I arrived one day to see Heidi sitting on the floor, looking in a three-way mirror, and singing to herself. The teacher was busy making popcorn and bagging it to raise money for the PTA. I asked her what method she was using to teach the students to read, so I could match it at home. I told her I'd used basic phonics for my other children and had taught both of them how to read myself. She revealed that she didn't use phonics or any reading methods because the students had no idea what reading was all about until they got into middle school! Needless to say, I was horrified! I went to the principal of the elementary school and told him about what was *not* being taught. While he listened to me, he really had nothing to say. When I left his office, I knew my doom was sealed when I saw a plaque in the hall with the name of the teacher who'd been voted the one with the "Most Professional Approach," whatever that meant! And yes, it was Heidi's teacher.

After this incident, I called Mary, the head of the special education department. We knew Mary from Heidi's participation in the program, and she took me to a school where there was a young teacher who had stations around the room for various learning activities. There was a table where students sat with the teacher for one-on-one time in learning their math and reading skills. There was also a place to sit where they could independently use a word machine.

Here's how the word machine worked. The children would insert a large card from the left, and, as it passed through, the machine said the word. It was fun and effective. What a great machine! In addition, there was a quiet corner for sitting on a beanbag and looking through books. There was also a math table where manipulatives were available and worksheets to go with them. I was astonished and speechless. Mary was sitting quietly off to the side and smiling at me as my mouth hung open. She asked me if I would like to see the rest of the building too. I told her that it didn't matter what the rest of the building looked like and asked, "Where can I sign on the dotted line?" Mary had brought me to one of the best teachers in the system.

In the end, Heidi attended that school in that classroom the following year. She blossomed in many ways and progressed from those basic functional words to some other, more important ones: different foods and drinks on restaurant menus!

···32···
Mom's Growing Up Too

I'm just a woman
Taking care of her.
Not much more clever
But at times I wish I were.

I'm a slow learner
In my own special ways.
It's taken time to clearly see...
There is growth in delays.

I finally figured out
That it really doesn't matter,
If the juice misses the cup
And on the floor does splatter

For what I see are trying hands
To buckle and to zip
Or tie those shoes once and for all—
Who says it must be quick?

It matters not
If the buttons aren't right
It only matters
She's always in His sight.

It matters not
That papers get torn
But that to us
Yes, she was born.

The smudges and accidents
That make me sigh
God says aren't worth
The fussing in my mind.

For all He sees
In her little heart
Is the courage she has
To make each new start.

Forgive me, Lord
My nearsightedness
May you impart to me
Your love and kindness.

···33···
Jumping Hannah, Hide-and-Seek, and Other Bedroom Stories

WHEN HEIDI GREW older and needed to wake up early for school, she soon decided that she would rather sleep in. Those early mornings were not fun for her or for me. This is the time to tell you about one more important member of the family. Her name was Hannah, she was our Siberian husky, and we all loved her. And one day, I realized the answer to our waking up struggle. Hannah would wake Heidi up, not me!

Here's a little background information on Hannah. Hannah was an amazing dog. She jumped over fences and bushes outside and could take all six steps up the front porch in a single bound. Woe to the person who accidentally got in the way. Once Hannah knocked down a little friend of ours during an innocent and joyful greeting. The boy went home unharmed but with Hannah's paw prints on the front of his shirt! In the springtime, she would charge around the house flinging up clods of new grass behind her. Once a neighbor yelled to me that she'd seen Hannah jump over the mailman (Well, he was short, but still.). I truly think Hannah had an identity crisis. She thought she was a deer or a gazelle. So, with all this power in mind, picture me calling for Hannah to come upstairs to wake up Heidi. I quickly jumped out of the way when we heard the pounding locomotive of sheer energy stampeding into Heidi's bedroom, leaping onto her bed, and then settling down next to Heidi, happily panting. Anyone else would have resented this wakeup call, but she loved it. Heidi would roll over to Hannah, put her arm around her, and say ever so sweetly, "Hi, Poochie! Hi, Hannah!" After a little while, Heidi would stop petting her and get up…happily.

In addition to our unique morning wakeup call, hide-and-seek also played a prominent role in our house. However, hide-and-seek is not a game I enjoy very much, especially when I can't find the hiding person, and Heidi wasn't always easy to find. I began to wonder if that was why I named her Heidi—because she was hiding all of the

Her Name Is Heidi

time. On one such occasion, Heidi didn't seem to be in the house at all, so we ventured outside. Now just because we called her name didn't mean that she answered. I think Heidi truly didn't think it was necessary. At any rate, we were calling away with no success, but we soon learned of her new, happy place. What better place than to be nestled in the sweet, fresh hay in Hannah's enclosed outside home? While it was cute to see her there, still, at these times, Heidi was definitely in the doghouse!

One significant hide-and-seek adventure involved Susan, who was babysitting the kids for a weekend. Upon not finding Heidi in her bed, Susan started the search. She looked *everywhere* to no avail, but Susan was not aware of Heidi's strange sleeping habits. If she had been, all of this frantic searching might not have happened. For example, one of Heidi's more common sleeping positions was on her knees with the rest of her still on the bed. It looked as though she was praying. Sometimes Heidi slept while hanging sideways off the bed: one arm and leg on and one arm and leg off. Sometimes she slid off the other side of the bed and became securely wedged between the bed and the wall. Andrew always loved seeing Heidi's latest sleeping position. You never knew what to expect. Well, just as Susan was getting frantic in her search, she looked under Heidi's bed and there she was! Heidi had managed to roll under the bed and was blissfully sound asleep! While it is fun to think back on, believe me, it was no laughing matter for Susan at the time.

···34···
Social Skills

ANOTHER ASPECT OF Heidi's elementary school was learning social skills. For instance, the teachers would model for students how to verbally confront others when they were mistreated. One day when I was visiting, I saw how the teachers taught them this using role-playing. This was a good activity for Heidi because she was quiet and not verbal when she needed to be.

The role-playing began, and each student took his or her turn saying, "No" at the appropriate time. Then it was Heidi's turn. The teachers asked her what she should say when someone was mean to her. She just stood there. We waited and waited. Finally, one of her close friends got up and started pulling on her shirtsleeve! The friend kept tugging and tugging, but Heidi just stood there. Finally Heidi yelled, "Stop it!" Everyone clapped and cheered, and she smiled.

The students were also taught to not interrupt a class but rather to raise their hand to participate. But there is more to participation than merely raising one's hand, and properly participating in group discussions by staying on topic is one of Heidi's least favorite pastimes. All throughout elementary school, middle school, and high school, we tried to get her to stay on topic. Even at her workplace after high school, Heidi was corrected about veering off topic in the middle of discussions. I am sorry to say that as even as an adult, Heidi still interrupts conversations with off topic ideas. I haven't figured out if she is not able to follow along with the train of thought, or if like some of us, she just zones out and then whatever comes to her mind then comes out of her mouth. Maybe it's lazy listening? We are still working on this, but, no matter who we are, don't we always have things to work on?

···35···
Class Mother

WHEN HEIDI STARTED attending her new elementary school, I decided to get involved in whatever the class was doing. As some of you know, often in special education classes there are students whose parents are not active in any way when it comes to their child's education. In Heidi's new class, there were three students whose parents had never even attended their Individualized Education Program (IEP) meetings, and these are important meetings where the school explains the supports and services it will provide to their child. This lack of involvement happens for a variety of reasons. Many are single parents, and many live in poverty. Hence, they are too busy just trying to get by and make enough money to feed and clothe their children.

After assessing the situation, I decided to offer my help and asked if the teacher would like for me to be the class mother. She just looked at me and said, "What's a class mother?" I was shocked but smiled in response. I told her that I would like to bake cupcakes for special parties and assist on field trips. The teacher just stood there with her mouth open. Once she recuperated, she said yes and asked if we could include the other special education class that had only about nine students. Of course!

For the next few years, I baked cookies and went on field trips. There was another mother who also took part in these occasions, and we became good friends, as our children did. We even look back on that time as some of the most fun experiences we ever had in school. We continued serving in the classroom through our children's middle school days, and Heidi loved it. When I eventually started working in a school as an instructional assistant, her heart was broken because I couldn't just show up to her classroom all of the time. Looking back, I don't remember how many times we went to the zoo, the metro parks, the libraries, or the Nutcracker, but we truly made our way around this city and were the better for it.

···36···
Camping

WE WENT CAMPING as a family each summer with our friend Vicky. It was an inexpensive way to get outside, and it was worth all the work. Heidi always loved the water and was always the first to dive in, without hesitation, no matter how cold it was. She is a good swimmer, if swimming underwater counts. That is the only way she swims, which, unfortunately, makes it difficult to see her for constant head checks. She thankfully also mastered doing summersaults in the water, which made her a bit more visible. With the addition of goggles, she even learned how to retrieve the weighted and colored toys off the bottom of the pool.

At one campground there was a very tall slide with water running down it, emptying into the lake. The water at the bottom of the slide was about three feet deep, so it was not over Heidi's head. Therefore, she decided to try it out. With Mom in the water at the bottom of the slide and Dad on the ladder behind her, she took the plunge. She zipped past me so quickly that I missed catching her! Under she went, and I was horrified! First, her feet popped up, and then a moment later, she sprang up out of the water, smiling, and laughing. The speed and plunging did not discourage her at all. Now she climbed the ladder all by herself, and Mom stayed at her waterslide post. She was very proud of herself and so were we.

Down in southern Ohio, we also went to a place called Indian Mound Campground. There was a little pond in which to swim, and Heidi loved to be there, even though the minnows nibbled our feet. We all enjoyed walking around the grounds and woods. There was a full-size Indian teepee next to the pond to sit in and enjoy. In the fall, they even had an old-fashioned pig roast, where everyone brought side dishes to share with all.

One of the more memorable experiences at Indian Mound Campground happened on the land slide. It was a turquoise plastic slide built into the hill. You had to climb a ladder to get to the platform at the top. This platform offered a fast and steep drop, which gave the necessary speed to arrive at the monstrous cushion at the end of the ride. Wax paper was offered to ensure a good ride, but sometimes even that didn't work so well. Heidi tried it but wasn't so thrilled about it. Her brother was another story, however. The Indian chief told us not to use water on the slide because some boys had done so and nearly killed themselves in the process. Well, we had never even thought of that! I hate to admit it, but now we did. What was a warning soon turned into a challenge. Good grief, what were we thinking? So, on a humid day, when the sliding was pretty slow and sticky, we actually let Andrew pour a bucket of water onto it and follow in quick pursuit. What we witnessed was amazing. He flew down the slide at break-neck speed. Not only did he arrive at the monstrous cushion, but he never even touched it. He flew over it and then disappeared out of sight, down the hill! We all stared, with mouths hanging open, and started calling out to him. A moment later he jumped up from down the hill, with arms pumped up over his head in victory. He was shouting all kinds of happy proclamations. The girls never wanted to try that, but Andrew still talks about his awesome air-born ride down that hill.

Old Man's Cave has also seen Heidi a number of times and at different ages. When she and Deborah were quite young, I put them both on leashes because I'd heard horror stories about people disappearing over the cliffs. We played in the falls and pools, and she loved it all, even as she grew older. "Top of the Caves Campground" had a swimming pool where Heidi tried her hardest to teach Vicky how to swim but to no avail. We just had to watch out for everyone in the pool and rescue Vicky when she had more courage than her ability warranted.

Campfires and hikes have been a part of Heidi's early days since she was very young. As an older person, she even became a faithful comrade on Mom's sailboat for a number of years. She was never afraid, always trusting us. Even when the wind was strong, the boat was rocking, and the waves were splashing on her, she would just tuck down under the bow and nestle in on the pile of life jackets. She even went to sleep there, once. A fearless sailor indeed! Land and sea have given Heidi a lot of exciting experiences and lessons in her life.

···37···
Family Church Camp

HEIDI AND MOM attend two church camps. One church camp goes all the way back to when Andrew was only two years old. This camp functioned by having classes for the children while the adults had their own meetings. My kids loved those classes because they had crafts and fun outdoor activities. I usually put Heidi in with Deborah, so Deborah could keep an eye on her.

One year, as Heidi grew older, I discovered that she had been placed with her own age group. This concerned me because it was the first time she'd ever been with her peers. I wondered how she could possibly keep up with the others. How did the teacher manage the situation? Well, I soon found out.

Heidi had done very well, and the other children had taken her under their wings. They gladly helped her with the crafts and assignments. Some of the kids would even walk up to me on the campground and proudly announce what Heidi had done that day in class, which made me smile.

I often walked away from these "reporters" scratching my head and wondering when Heidi had grown up so quickly. She was keeping up with her own grade group, which revealed that I wasn't keeping up with Heidi! She was ahead of her mom.

> When a baby is one, they usually walk
> When a baby is two, they usually talk.
> When a baby is three, they run and climb
> When a child is four, they forever hide.
>
> When a child is five, their letters they learn
> When a child is six, to school, it's their turn.
> When a child is seven, he asks about heaven
> When a child is eight, he wants to stay up late.
>
> When a child is nine, we see that it's time
> For them to live their lives, "cuz it's mine."
> Special ones don't fit this mold
> Parents are unfortunately told…
>
> That something is wrong…it makes one feel blue
> But let's focus on the good, keep a positive tune.
> Let's see who they are and what they can do…
> And even sometimes, what they do for YOU!
>
> They make us all grow and eventually see
> That being human is the best thing to be.
> Most of all, they're special in God's sight,
> His dear ones, so precious, to Him a delight.

···38··· What Do Others Think?

What do others think?
I wondered when she was a babe.
These thoughts often filled my heart
And tainted many a day.

What do they think?
As I'm walking down the street,
Fears and worries would arise
As new strangers I would meet.

What do they think?
I would quickly search their face.
I could tell if they were struggling
And I'd want to walk away.

Bonnie Elder

What are they thinking?
I don't hear this much anymore.
I have other things to think about
And to worry, I can't afford.

To care or even be concerned
About those others in my life,
Is not a problem anymore
For I know she is a delight.

If others cannot see it,
It does not cause me any strife
For now I know even more so,
He brought her into my life.

••• 39 •••
Tonsillectomy???

JUST LIKE ANY other small child, Heidi had LARGE tonsils. Since there was a lot of strep throat going around, the doctor decided it was a good time to take hers out. No problem, right? Wrong. When it comes to Heidi, anything that should be routine is hardly *ever* routine, and this was no exception.

I agreed to the surgery, and for once, I thought of something practical. Heidi had been born with an extra little "thumb" on her thumb. It really wasn't that big, but that's what we called it. Apparently, it was bothering her because she kept chewing on it. So, I asked the doctor if, while she was unconscious, they could remove that little tag, and he arranged for the appropriate doctor to do so.

Shortly after entering the operating room, the doctor came out and told us that Heidi's breathing passage was so small that they couldn't get the tube down her throat for the anesthesia. They weren't sure why her breathing passage was so little, but they couldn't even fit in the tiniest tube that they use for infants! Thus, for the time being, there was no option of doing the tonsillectomy.

I told the doctor that she'd had trouble breathing ever since her open-heart surgery, and he revealed that scar tissue might have grown over her breathing passage because a tube had been there for so long after her surgery. We ended up keeping Heidi in the hospital to observe her breathing, and it grew worse. The medical staff had to bring intensive care into her room because the ICU was full. A few days later, Heidi didn't even respond to the oxygen tent or mask. As a matter of fact, Heidi was begging for the mask, which she didn't even used to like. Our pediatrician friend came to visit, and I could see the worry on his face. I asked what they would have to do if they couldn't help her breathing. He told me honestly that they might have to give her a tracheotomy, and I was devastated.

I'd seen many children with them and had always hoped we would never have to experience one. It seemed as though this was my crucible, as an ugly enemy came to call again. I lay down on the long window seat and sobbed quietly to myself. When I stopped crying, this is what I prayed: "Lord? I realize that Heidi may need this, and I'm willing to go through it, if it is Your will, but I'm asking, please don't require this of me."

By this time, Heidi was like a large, wet noodle draped over my arms, and she was growing unresponsive. The outlook didn't seem good. A new nurse came in as the shifts changed and was alarmed at Heidi's condition. She told me that I could demand to see a doctor, so I did. A resident and intern arrived, and I asked if anything was going to be done. They replied that a doctor would be in the next morning who would then decide what to do. Needless to say, I was livid by then and said very loudly, "There may not be a tomorrow morning! Look at her! I call this child abuse!" Bingo! I had said the right words. They looked at each other in alarm, said they'd be right back, and sure enough they were. They gave me papers to sign, and Heidi was whisked off to an emergency cauterization of the scar tissue. Her throat was somewhat swollen from all the attempts of getting the tube down, and she needed help *now*. Still, one of the options written on the form was the dreaded tracheotomy, so we were not yet out of the woods. We again called the church, and surprisingly about fifteen people showed up in the upstairs lobby. As we waited, it was quiet and tense.

Her Name Is Heidi

I had no idea that Heidi would return on the elevator right where we were waiting, but she did. We heard the "ding" of the elevator and all turned around to see who it is. Lo and behold, it was Heidi on her wheeled bed. Was she gasping for breath? Was she lying in a pitiful heap and hooked up to an IV? Nope. She was sitting up and looking at all of us with a ticked-off expression that said, "What are you all looking at?" She was mad, so I knew she was well, and her breathing was completely normal—without a tracheotomy.

The elevator surprise was so astonishing and she looked so cute that many of us had to hide our giggles and smiles, which made her even angrier. Heidi came through, once more, against the odds, floating on prayers and her hospital bed. She was ready to go home!

···40···
Special Olympics

AFTER ALL OF the sickness and slow beginnings in so many ways, it was hard to believe that Heidi had made it ten years. But here she was, active, slimming out, and looking more grown-up. At this point, she still liked to wear pretty dresses, tights, and new shoes. She liked to comb her hair and the hair of other little girls, and she enjoyed playing on her new computer. This was also the year she started the Special Olympics, the largest sport organization in the world!

The first sport Heidi started in was track and field. She was fast and earned many medals for running. She even had her picture in the local paper. The photo was taken during a practice session as she came across the finish line with her arms up in the air and a victorious smile on her face. Despite her running success, the softball throw was truly her forte because Heidi had developed a strong pitching arm from playing ball with her big brother. The judges would stand where they thought Heidi's ball would land, but it always sailed over their heads. She threw it forty or fifty feet even when she was little, and Andrew stood by proudly watching.

Her Name Is Heidi

The next sport Heidi tried was gymnastics. While the routine was too hard for her to remember, we still had a good year trying it out. Next up was bowling, which became her favorite sport, and for a while she often scored between 130 and 150, beating her mother. This lasted many years until she decided she would rather sleep in on Saturdays, and I couldn't blame her. Last of all was bocce. Heidi and her partner won gold medals in the state competition two years in a row. She has, to date, 26 medals displayed in shadow boxes in her room.

After a few years, bocce began to lose its appeal. There are so many rounds to play that the waiting really began to bother Heidi, and she said, "Why is this taking so long?" Overall, bocce just took up more time than any other sport. For example, the athletes would start before the opening exercises and not finish until mid-afternoon. Sometimes that meant long hours spent in the hot sun, which was also not good for her. I felt badly when I saw her unhappiness with bocce. I told my own mother about it, and she said something very wise: "I thought this was something that she was supposed to enjoy." That did it. I knew that from then on, I would let Heidi decide whether she wanted to play bocce anymore.

The last time Heidi played bocce at an area meet was one that I will always remember. Somehow, five volunteers didn't show up for the afternoon rounds, which meant there wouldn't have been a way to finish the competition. What were we to do? They made an announcement, asking for people to help, and our *entire* family stood up and walked over to the judges' table to offer our services!

Slathered with sunscreen, we headed out onto the field armed with tape measures, score sheets, and a five-minute refresher course to take over the world. I was so proud of us! Deborah was with another group of scorers, and I saw her helping to position the balls in the right places at the start of each round. Jeff was given the tape measure to officially record the distance between the balls. Andrew and I kept track of scores and lined up contestants. At the end of the day, none of the games had to be forfeited, and while we were sunburned and exhausted, we were also happy as we turned in our equipment. We had done it! As Andrew commented, it was better than just sitting out there in the hot sun waiting for things to happen, and it also concluded Heidi's last year of bocce and time with the Special Olympics.

···41···
Up North

WE HAD FRIENDS who owned three cabins on Shupac Lake, a little body of water about five driving hours north of Toledo. As a child I had visited there with my parents and brother, and now we were invited to bring our own children there each summer. The lake was crystal clear, and it was said to be bottomless in places. That always scared me as a child, but we all swam in it anyway. There were springs feeding into the lake, which made it extremely cold. For this reason, we visited at the end of August or else it was too cold to swim and too cold in general.

At the lake there were also little dingys to sail, a catamaran, a canoe, a wind surfer, a fishing boat at the dock, and a raft for the brave-hearted to swim to. Mr. Brand, the owner of the territory, was a great teacher of boating, flying kites, making things out of wood in his workshop, and just about anything else we wanted to do. He also taught us about sailing by using a model boat set on a dining table as a fan blew into it. He was a self-taught sailor, but since he was also a lawyer, he had a way of talking that kept the kids riveted.

Then there was the music that played on an old Victrola, songs like, "Barney Google," "Stewball Was a Race Horse," and "Yes, We Have No Bananas." My son used to think I was teasing him about these songs until he heard them himself after the phonograph was wound up by the crank handle.

Heidi enjoyed our time up north. She was fascinated with the little fish under the dock and would lie down on the dock to study them. Mr. Brand came up with a great, handmade discovery tool that helped her with her studies. He cut the top and bottom out of a large coffee tin and covered the bottom with plastic kitchen wrap. He showed her how to hold it on the water, just enough to make the fish clear. It was a wonderful invention and left Heidi there for hours as she enjoyed the unsuspecting fish. Heidi also liked to go out sailing in the dingy with me—she has always enjoyed being on the water with her mother. She even enjoyed bailing out the fishing boat!

One day I couldn't figure out where Heidi had gone until we saw her on the lake in the rowboat—all by herself! Needless to say, I was frantic, but Mr. Brand, true to character, was not ruffled in the least. He noted that she had put on a life jacket, so she had done what needed to be done. We all went down to the boathouse while Mr. Brand sat on his beach chair in the sand, equipped with his swimming suit on and pipe in mouth. I watched in amazement as he very patiently coached Heidi to shore. It went something like this:

OK, now pull with the other oar...
All right, now pull with the other arm...
Good, now pull with the other one...
And on an on.

Mr. Brand was not upset or mad; he just kept telling her what to do next. After all, as he'd said, he had helped a number of children and grandchildren master the water. By this point, I was smiling and muttering to myself about his patience. In the end, Heidi was rather proud of herself bringing in the boat and so was I!

···42···
Dairy Queen Treats

ONE HOT SUMMER day when Heidi was a teenager, we decided to go out and enjoy a cool treat. We ordered our ice cream and sat down at a picnic table to enjoy them. I was not paying attention to Heidi or whatever else was going on, but suddenly I heard her say, "What are you looking at?"

I quickly turned to see to whom she was speaking. There was a man sitting at the table next to us, and, apparently, he had been watching her. With no hesitation he responded, "I was looking at your pretty eyes." While I thought his words were so sweet, Heidi was not impressed. She simply turned back to her Dairy Queen treat. To be honest, I was amazed to see Heidi advocating for herself. She knew it was rude to stare at others, and she had defended herself. This is the only time I have ever heard her do so, and what a joy it was to see!

Our ice cream outing reminds me that there are people who feel inadequate when they meet someone with a disability—some of my best friends have told me even they do! And this happens to people

Her Name Is Heidi

all over the world. Once a minister from Brazil met Heidi at a large church conference, and here were his thoughts on the matter:

I was raised in Brazil, a culture where the people with deficiencies are hidden from view. Therefore, I have not learned to interact with them in a completely prejudice-free and authentic, loving way as a disciple of Jesus ought to do. The fear of being caught feeling sore instead of loving them unconditionally has held me back for quite a long time, for I realized that my true feelings would become transparent to them. So, I avoided them and in doing so, my ministry suffered and I was not complete.

The first person to help me with this was Heidi, a young girl, probably 12 or 13, to whom I got to give some hugs throughout the week of the church world conference. At the end of the week, she came running to me with a big smile to give me a hug. It made me cry for joy. This was God's way to let me know that I have indeed overcome my fears and that His love flowing through me was made real to her.

This Brazilian minister was absolutely right about Heidi's ability to correctly perceive that his love for her was genuine. In fact, Heidi can tell instantly if someone loves her, and boy does she respond! She can also tell if others want to spend time with her or not. I remember a statement spoken by another mother of a handicapped child, and her words are both funny and very serious: "My daughter may be retarded, but she ain't no fool!" I have said that to some of my friends, and they laugh because they know it is true about Heidi. She can even stump me or fool me into thinking she can't do certain things that she really can. I am still working on understanding her in this way. As our friend Thelma has said, Heidi just doesn't want people to know how smart she is. A lot of people don't realize she has this ability to see through them and gauge their heart towards her. They think they can fool her, but she ain't no fool! I suppose this is how she can teach us a thing or two about real love.

···43···
Middle School

HEIDI'S MIDDLE SCHOOL was a great experience for all of us. Again, we hit it right with the teacher, and Heidi was academically challenged and treated well. She made friends there that followed her through high school and beyond. It was also during those middle school years that I continued to go on field trips with her class, and another mother, her son, and I all became good friends.

At this point, she was still involved in the Special Olympics. Heidi also thoroughly enjoyed playing foursquare during recess and went on many wonderful field trips. Her IEP (Individual Educational Plan) continued her progress in reading, math, and functional skills. In addition, Heidi had to learn how to sit in a study hall and work on some of her assignments. She even participated in art and music and attended all of the school assemblies.

After the rough start in elementary school, thankfully things turned out well in middle school. Heidi even was able to participate in some home economics and shop classes before the school closed down those programs. There were many opportunities at the time, and all of my children benefitted from them. Happy days!

···44···
Over the Wall

A MOTHER OF a boy with Down's syndrome was on TV. She was being interviewed and shared a story about how, one day, her son came home and asked her, "When will it go away?" She asked him what he was talking about, and he replied, "The way I am." What a heartrending, insightful, teenaged plea! What could she possibly say? It wasn't going to go away, and she couldn't pretend that it would. There are days when I know that Heidi knows she is different. Sometimes it comes from how others look at her or speak to her. Sometimes she just gets hurt, and sometimes she speaks up for herself. She knows what they are thinking. One time she said to me, "No one will play with me." These are just a few of the daily difficulties that Heidi faces. Maybe she gets tired of it, like I do. Maybe she gets discouraged about it, like I do. Maybe she wishes it will go away, even if she doesn't say so.

How do we proceed in life when we are facing a wall and we just can't get around it, over it, or even under it? This struggle is about me, Heidi's mom. I had found myself up against such a wall and had come to a standstill. I was stuck in a rut. I couldn't get into a positive mindset. I felt as though I couldn't go on being her mother. Sometimes I told people that God gave Heidi the wrong mother. They would smile and tell me that was not true, but I was worn out and all vision was gone.

I decided to share this inner grappling with our home group. I told my friends how much I was struggling, how I'd come to my standstill. Then they gathered around me for prayer. They all prayed for me, and at the end, the last friend prayed, "Lord, Bonnie has come up against a wall. Lord, lift her up above that wall and place her feet on the Rock, which is You. Give her new faith; bring her from faith to faith." As those words were spoken, in my mind I saw myself being lifted up to the top of that wall and standing on the Rock. I felt it in my spirit. It lifted my spirit, and I was able to move forward. It was such a good reminder that we aren't supposed to go through life on our own. Once again, it was prayer from others that got me through.

···45···
To Come to You

To come to You, my Lord
It hurts me to the very core
I want to say, stop hurting me
Yet to You I must come for more...
More of the Living Water
More of Your peace for my soul
More of Your love and faithfulness
More testings to make me whole.

To come to You, my Lord
Kills all the evil within.
I cannot continue to linger
In resentment, selfishness, and sin.

Bonnie Elder

To come to You, my Lord
Is as humbling as can be.
I see myself so needy
Yet still You say, "Come to Me."

To come to You, my Lord
Is different from yesterday.
It's not as easy for me to do,
After the past several days.

To come to You, my Lord
I hesitate; it's true.
Yet where else can I possibly go?
For there is only life in You.

···46···
Finding Providers

WHEN I WAS going back to college to become a teacher, I needed help with Heidi. It wasn't that she was a bother to me; it was just that she was bored, sitting at home and watching Mom study, and I can't blame her. I was told by friends who were care providers that Heidi was "too high functioning" to receive services from places like Respite or other organizations. I believed them, so I didn't call.

During my classes to become an Intervention Specialist (Special Education Teacher), I had to read a book that discussed the best cases of care providers for special needs children. The more I read, the angrier I became. Where were these services for my daughter? For example, there was a blind boy who was living this wonderful, fulfilled life on a farm, where people helped him get to the barn to pick eggs out of the chickens' nests. He was so happy, and so was everyone else involved. There were three other cases I had to read about, and it was about all I could do to get through the material without blowing up.

My instructor then said she had an assignment for us. She wanted us to seek out a service that would help one of our students at school. That did it! I raised my hand and said, "How can I do that when I haven't been able to find services for my own daughter?" She looked at me and could tell I was mad. She responded, "Alright, then your assignment is to find services for your daughter," which satisfied me. I had some pamphlets and paperback books from some organizations that proudly announced their wonderful services and was ready to seek them out.

For three days, I got on the phone and called various organizations. I contacted the Council For Mentally Retarded Citizens and talked to its founding mother. She was a delightful person and understood my plight. However, the services only covered extracurricular activities to which I would have to transport Heidi myself. As kind as the woman was, we never took advantage of the organization because it would have been more work for me. The organization finally disbanded due to the fact that there were so many other organizations offering the same services. Still, it had been founded around fifty years ago and was a pioneer in the field, serving the community well when no one else knew there were handicapped people in the world.

Big Brothers and Big Sisters didn't serve handicapped people; plus, Heidi was too old. And while there were many, many organizations that would have been options, there was a catch—we would have been penniless if we had signed up. I thought it was strange. How could anyone pay that kind of money? For example, there is a wonderful camp experience called Recreation Unlimited within driving distance of Columbus. However, the cost for a weekend was beyond what I was willing to pay (around $400.00, I believe). While Heidi's Level One Waiver (her government funding) could pay for it, the cost would use up her funding very quickly, leaving her without any other options.

What did I discover at the end of my three days of frustration? Well, I decided to call the County Respite even though my well-meaning friends had told me Heidi would not qualify for their services. I talked to the lead person and spilled my guts. I told her I was a single parent who was going back to school and working as well. I told her I was exhausted and tired of not getting help for Heidi. She acknowledged that I did, indeed, need help. *Yes!* Finally someone had heard my desperate plea, and I couldn't believe it! She set up an appointment to come to my place. She revealed that Respite usually comes to the home to take care of clients in order to give the parent a break, time to go to the store, and so on. I explained that I didn't need someone to come to my home, but, rather, I needed someone to take Heidi *out* of the home, to the YMCA to exercise, to go watch a movie, or to eat out. Thankfully, she decided my need was big enough to serve us in such a way.

At first, Heidi was shy about being with people she didn't know. As always, some of the care providers worked out better than others, but we finally came up with Tonia who Heidi grew to love and adore. She spent time with Tonia two or three days a week. It was wonderful, and we were all happy. Heidi was about 25 years old at this time, and it was a much-needed service that was way too late in coming. Still, I was grateful and happy for Heidi's broadening horizons.

The County Respite was the only thing I had found during my three-day, traumatic search with my ear stuck to the phone, but I was grateful for the professor's homework assignment. By the way, the service's expenses were based on family income, so my bill was very small. Bingo! I won in both ways with Respite. God was clearly still watching over me, as He always does.

···47···
A Game-Changing Day

SITTING ON A cement wall and watching Heidi compete in bocce brought more than the normal amount of satisfaction to my life one fateful day. A gentleman sitting next to me had been obviously noticing my cheers and normal, noisy support of Heidi's endeavors when he turned to me and asked if I was Heidi's mother. I have found that question springing up more and more as I get older and have grown more and more confused about it. "Of course!" I am thinking, "Who else would act like this at a competition?" But instead, I politely say, "Yes."

He proceeded to introduce himself as the manager of a private homecare organization. He told me they take care of people like Heidi, by having staff come to the home and assist her in learning basic homemaking skills such as cooking, cleaning, personal hygiene, and more. All I could think was, "Oh, great! *Another* person to take care of in my home!" (I told him that too.) I also shared that I didn't think Heidi would enjoy working all day and then having to work an additional two hours in the home. Rather, we needed someone to take Heidi *out* of the home. He listened, then told me to think about it, and gave me his card. I also gave him my name and number, and I am glad I did! He didn't give up on me, and even though it was a year or two later, he convinced me to give them a try. I did, and it was a good thing for both of us.

Heidi met her first care provider and off they went! They visited the YMCA to workout, took walks, and ate out if they wanted. They saw each other five days a week, and Heidi loved it. Our other provider's hours had dropped from three times a week to once a month, so this filled in the gap. I was also sick at this time, so they took over going to the grocery store and fixing food for our dinners when I just didn't have the strength. What a blessing! I finally started having some respite for *me*. Since I was still working, it was nice to have the extra help. Once again, God was taking care of us in very detailed ways.

···48···
Allowances

IT SEEMS THAT, just like any other child, Heidi was not exactly motivated to do chores, but she had more free time than I did. I was working and taking classes to earn a teaching license in special education. As a result, I had classes twice a week after work. At that time, we were living in a small apartment, so upkeep was easy.

I shared our dilemma with another teacher who worked with special education students. He recommended giving Heidi an allowance. I had never thought about it, so I started giving Heidi $20.00 per week. She was worth it, and I was thrilled. So, Heidi did the dishes, cleaned out the cat litter box, and vacuumed. The part that made her chores fun was going to the Laundromat down the hall. She was able to put quarters in the machines, which was so much fun for her! She also took the clothesbaskets down, loaded them, dried them, and hung the clothes up on the hangers. Nobody ever bothered her, and it was a wonderful service to us.

I once heard a story about an elderly man who was having trouble taking care of himself. He had a daughter who had Down's syndrome, and she took care of him—she really did! Heidi has been known to bring me tea or toast when I am sick. Plus, I know she could do more if needed. I have told her that someday she might be taking care of me, but she just looks at me to see if I am kidding or not. Why would she do that? Because she knows that sometimes I joke with her. Still, this is one thing I am not joking about. While I hope it doesn't come to that, someone will have to do it, and Heidi is quite capable.

···49···
The Fish Fry and Crashing Parties

HEIDI NEVER CEASES to amaze me by how quickly she can get involved in *any* situation. Our friends had introduced us to church fish frys during Lent, and we became faithful customers. We were at our favorite location, and I was away from the table when I heard the winning lottery ticket being announced. It was the first announcement of our stay, but I really didn't pay too much attention because we never bought lottery tickets.

Arriving back at our table, I noticed Heidi wasn't there. When I asked my friends where she was, they pointed to the announcer and said, "Heidi was asked to pick a lottery ticket, and they announced that hers was the winning ticket!" I looked over and saw a huge smile on her face, and she was jumping up and down. The man was smiling at her, as they took her picture! Oh, boy, that was even more exciting. She came running back to our table and said, "Mommy, I won!" Sure enough, she had two dollars in her hand. She was so excited and was laughing all at once. Of course, she proceeded to take one dollar and buy herself a soft drink. This experience showed me, again, how easily Heidi could talk to strangers and be completely comfortable. Plus, it made the evening worthwhile.

Her fish fry winning experience reminded me of how quickly Heidi could get herself into fun adventures, without the assistance of her mother. For example, once at a bowling alley, we were just about to leave when a mom came up to her and said, "Hi, Heidi! My daughter is having her birthday party now. Would you like to come over?" Well, of course she did! She had cake and ice cream and generously gave a $5.00 bill on her own accord. She knew that was the right thing to do.

However, Heidi's next adventure was not quite as honest, but somehow she can manage to crash parties with grace and ease and escape condemnation. This time, we went to her favorite arcade, the Buckeye Café. As we entered the front doors, it said, "Closed. Private Party." I couldn't believe it! This had never happened before. Dread descended upon me, and I looked at Heidi and explained to her that it was a private party, which meant we couldn't play there that night. The hostess just looked at us, and we looked back at her. Then Heidi said, "I have to go to the bathroom!" When she has to go, she has to go! I asked permission from the hostess, and off we tromped towards the back of the cafe to the girls' room.

Her Name Is Heidi

When we exited the bathroom, we were already halfway to the arcade. Heidi simply headed to the arcade like she always did, and I followed her, saying we really shouldn't be there. She didn't see the problem. To her, it was natural; to me, I was a guilty convict. The next thing you know, we made our way into the arcade, and it was so full of people that I was afraid of losing her. I thought we could be honest about being there by sitting in one of the booths, ordering food and drink, and paying for it. Then I realized they would know we were imposters, since there was a picnic-style buffet already provided. I know I should have just dragged her out, but I didn't. Well, you can guess the rest.

Nobody knew us, and we knew nobody. It was too late to convince Heidi about the morality of the situation, and I figured that it really didn't hurt anybody to be there. So, I put on a smile, and we lined up with everybody else, had a hot dog and a drink, and sat down. As we munched on our stolen meal, I couldn't believe we had done it! Heidi tore off and played the machines as happy as a lark. I looked at her and marveled that we had actually crashed a party and succeeded.

···50···
My Sister Heidi

THIS IS ANDREW. Heidi is four years younger than me, and she is four years older than Deborah. The middle child. There's probably some psychological prediction of what the typical middle child's personality will be like, but that does not apply here. There is nothing typical about Heidi Michelle Billow.

When I heard that my sister was to be born, I was ecstatic to have someone to play with. Little did I know how long it would be until we would play together as most brothers and sisters do. Heidi had two heart surgeries before she was able to walk, and I can honestly say that I didn't know how long the two of us would have together or if her life would be cut short. I recall having to be creative and adaptive with the games we played. She was very weak physically in her younger years and behind her peers developmentally, but she and I improvised.

Heidi also does what she wants, when she wants, and doesn't ever have to give an explanation. The rest of us can't get away with that. If she is asked to mop the floor by Mom, she takes as much time as she can to do it or will simply ignore you. She makes excuses, says nothing, or maybe just makes a grunt or releases an exasperated sigh that says, "Leave me alone. I'll get to it later."

Heidi knew how to read (whole words) for quite a while before the rest of us ever knew. However, one day she let the cat out of the bag. We were all sitting in the living room, and she read a holiday card out loud. I exclaimed, "Heidi, you can read!" Then immediately with a look of humorous disgust and a smile, I also said, "She's had us fooled all along!" She knew if she let everyone know about her reading capacity that more would be expected of her. I imagine she didn't want to live up to all those expectations.

Heidi has always kept us laughing in both her younger years and adult years with her childlike exuberance. She gets very excited over any and every birthday, holiday, work party, retirement party—you name it. If there's food and drinks, she gets pumped up. Birthdays are particularly important to her. She plans and talks about her birthday eleven months in advance or pretty much as soon as hers has passed. While many people hate to be sung to in public, that is not Heidi. She loves it and welcomes it. Sometimes I think her idea of a perfect birthday would be visiting restaurants all day long and having the staff sing to her and bring out a dessert.

In her younger years, her affection for strangers concerned our family, even though it never caused any problems. I think it was mainly our family that was uncomfortable with the hugs she would give to strangers, especially men. Yet Heidi and the receiver of the hug seemed to be fine. Those who receive her affection, I believe, can tell she is genuine, and that's what makes it okay and comfortable in the moment.

It's also important to note that Heidi seems to know someone no matter where we go, whether it is a bowling alley, a restaurant, or even the McDonald's drive-through. More people know my sister Heidi than know our whole family put together. For our family, she has been and continues to be a blessing that God knew we needed.

··· 51 ···
Dr. Jekyll and Mr. Hyde

SINCE ANDREW HAS opened a can of worms about Heidi's "other" side, this seems to be a good place for this part of our story. All of the things I have written about her so far are completely true, as are the things I will share now.

It is true that Heidi loves to listen to worship CDs at home and is often moved by those songs. It is true that she makes people smile and laugh. It is true that she can break up a bad mood in the home with a simple comment. However, it is also true that she can be very rude by not answering people when they greet her. In addition, she interrupts conversations because she is not listening. Even though she's told her behavior is rude, she is kind of on her own wavelength. And while she has become upset when a friend at work didn't respond to her greeting, she doesn't think about how it hurts others when she does the same thing. So, socially, she is deficient in conversations. It embarrasses me and frustrates me as well. For example, she can act as though she doesn't know somebody who she has known for years! I think it is a combination of not knowing how to follow a conversation and also not caring. Sometimes people ask me a question about her and I respond, "Well, that depends on whether she is 3 or 33 on that day." Of course, she is wrapped up in her perspective of life—it is the only one she has. Aren't we all this way? Still, it is no excuse to have to keep correcting her when she hurts others' feelings.

At other times, Heidi might get me a cup of tea or crackers if she sees I am not feeling well. She even worries about me if I can't get off the couch, which worries me too! Sometimes she can go beyond herself in these ways. But for those of you who are already acquainted with Heidi or another soul with a similar disability, you know that, at times, a type of two-sidedness is there.

Changing schedules is a set up for a bad moment or even bad day with Heidi. We all struggle with change. I know I do and even more so as I get older. However, when a special event is in store and it gets dashed to pieces, Heidi falls into pieces too. There are times when I am able to successfully console her and even provide an alternative. But other times, that is not possible, and we are both miserable.

Her Name Is Heidi

Dealing with these problems that occur when raising a special needs child, I remember the words of another parent that I read in a newsletter. The mother was trying to keep her child alive by not letting her cross the street. The child, not surprisingly, wanted to cross the street on her own, not being aware of the dangers involved. So, the mother would take hold of her hand and once back in their yard, she would tell her again not to do this and spank her. This became a repeated offense, much to the consternation of the mom and the pitiful pleas of her child. Of course, this was long enough ago, and spanking was considered the proper way to turn a wayward child around and not a thing of child abuse, worth imprisonment. Anyway, the mother noticed that when this occurred, she would look up just in time to see the neighbor's curtains quickly closing and wondered if she would be reported. We could ask why she spanked in public instead of taking her inside, but nonetheless, her lesson from the experience was this: society would tolerate a misbehaved special needs child, but they would not tolerate a special needs adult! Thus, fortified with this truth, she continued to save her daughter's life and ensure that she would happily live many years to come. The neighbor never did report her.

Another struggle sometimes occurs after work. Sitting on the couch after a long day of work and playing on her IPad or watching movies is Heidi's relax mode. I can't blame her for taking a break, but after a few hours on the couch, there are times when things need to be done. That's when the rubber meets the road. Those moments are when I am not very happy with my daughter.

I once read a story about a teenage girl who had to write a paper for a class in school. She decided to do a study on people with Down's syndrome because her sister had Down's syndrome and she wanted to learn more about it. After much research and writing, she came to her mother with the results. She told her mom that people who had Down's syndrome tended to be stubborn. The mother turned to her daughter and replied, "I could have saved you a lot of time and told you that myself."

··· 52 ···
Extended School Years

ACCORDING TO THE law, the Columbus City Schools could serve Heidi until she was 22 years old, which all kind of "accidentally" happened anyway. When she was in elementary school and her IEP was written at the end of the year, the teacher accidentally added that Heidi would repeat the fifth grade. We realized the mistake before signing the documents, but as I thought about it, I decided it was a good idea. Heidi was so short, gentle, and unable to defend herself. I figured that another year to learn some self-defense wouldn't hurt her at all. After all, what was the hurry to graduate at eighteen? Also in middle school, she was held back a year. I am not so sure this is allowed anymore, but it happened.

While in high school, she mostly attended the career center, where she did all kinds of activities in the community, and it was very beneficial work preparation for her adult life. She was at the career center so much that when she graduated, I am not sure she actually remembered where her high school was! Heidi had a work-study coordinator who helped suggest and place Heidi in the different programs available to her. Back then, Columbus had so many options and so many career centers (4) that each were in a different part of the city. She participated in office programs that included filing, shredding, making badges, collating, and filing envelopes.

In addition, Heidi worked in food service for the schools downtown, which was a fun job for her. She worked on the "assembly line," putting ketchup and mustard on the trays they passed her, and she kept up with it! She also opened boxes with desserts, such as Little Debbies, and placed them in a larger box to be put in separate meals. The career center also took them to the Shrine Temple across the street, and her class did the collating for their fall mailing as there were 10,000 letters going all over the entire state. The students were seated around the fez-shaped table in a fancy meeting room with bright green carpet. At the end of that mailing, the Shriners treated everyone to a big pizza party, and the kids were all happy about it.

Next up on the work experience was the city's Meals on Wheels. Heidi worked on the bread machine, which wrapped each piece of bread individually, and it had to be watched to make sure it didn't get stuck. Wearing her hairnet, she stayed on duty as a good worker should. She even worked at other food businesses, such as the Ocean

Club where she weighed the bags of pasta. Cheryl's Cookies enjoyed Heidi's helping to clean the glass displays, and being rewarded with a nice, big cookie was good enough for her.

Another opportunity opened at JoAnn Fabrics. The students packed their lunches and walked over for a full day of volunteering. They worked with a supervisor in the backroom to unpack merchandise. After eating their lunches and working a few hours in the afternoon, they walked back to the career center. It was a good experience of working a full day and sticking to it.

Hospital work offered another job where Heidi did very well and made many friends. The local Riverside Hospital let the students come and do different jobs in different locations. They started at the annex, which was on the other side of the road. One morning, I decided to go and "shadow" her. I arrived in time to follow Heidi as she made her way to her workstation, all by herself. Then we went downstairs to an underground passage that led us to the

Her Name Is Heidi

main hospital building. There were turns, more turns, and mirrors on the walls at some of the corners. We walked on and on and on, and I was so impressed with her sense of direction. Finally, we arrived at an X-ray room.

Heidi's job at the hospital was to fold small washcloths and hand towels and then put them on the wheeled cart for the patients. She did a great job, and the supervisor was so taken by her. When Heidi told her that she had a husky dog at home, the woman bought her a huge, stuffed husky dog to take home. She eventually stopped working there because, apparently, there were people with bruises who were quite sick, and this bothered Heidi. She has a sensitive spirit and seeing people in pain is hard on her. There were two other times when she was offered a job at nursing homes, but it upset her too much so she declined.

Finally, in the special education building of Columbus City Schools, there was a great job available to alphabetize. There were so many files since Columbus serves 60,000 students, and the special education population is not quite 10% of that group. There was a plastic filing invention that worked so cleverly to enable the students to do the job. The invention had each letter of the alphabet extended on a plastic stick that was all attached to a center spine. As long as the students knew their letters, they could be a big help to the office staff there. The staff would take the stack once the kids were done, file them, and let the kids start all over again. It was another fun time for Heidi to do a job that helped the school.

···53···
The Workshop

AFTER GRADUATING FROM high school in 2005, Heidi made her way into a workshop. That was one of the last years that the school gave "social" diplomas, which said she had completed a course of study at her high school. So, after graduation, she moved on to working in a workshop.

The workshop is divided into different areas, work or leisure, for their clients. Heidi has always wanted to work and make money. For many of her years there, Heidi was only paid in piecemeal style, resulting in very small checks. Finally things changed, and now she is paid $3.00 per hour. Her biweekly checks are between $70.00 and $90.00, which is still not much, but it's better than before.

When she first arrived at the workshop, there was not much work to do. On non-production days, the instructors offered alternative activities for the clients. While Heidi didn't like these activities, it was better than sitting at home. Then a job came from a company downtown that has kept the workshop happily employed ever since.

Her Name Is Heidi

The transportation to and from work has been a big blessing for me. Heidi is picked up at 8:30 a.m. and brought home at 2:45 p.m. At first she was picked up in a yellow bus like school children, which she enjoyed. Now she is picked up in a new, white van and likes that even more. She feels high class in the new van that her instructor drives.

Her service coordinator in high school always told me that Heidi was made for bigger things than working in a workshop. That might be true, but Heidi likes where she is. She is making money, has transportation, and has close supervision, which I feel is critical. It's a win-win situation, and whatever makes Heidi happy and keeps her active, I am all for it.

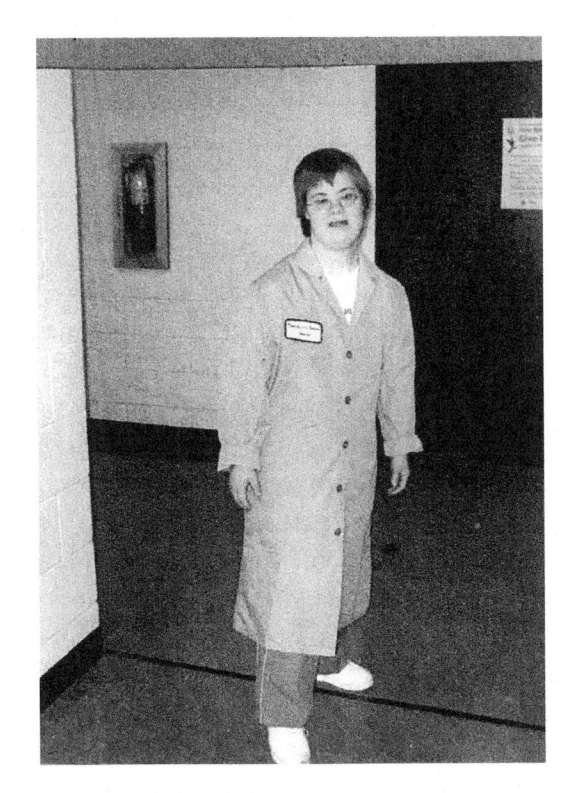

···54···
Technology Girl

NOW THAT HEIDI is in her thirties, she has surprised me in a new way. When I asked her what she wanted for Christmas one year, she said a cell phone. I couldn't have been more surprised! She just likes to use it for telling time or calling different family members if we are apart, which I like as well. She has learned how to use the camera on it and has taken pictures that are quite nice! She has also somehow saved the pictures from many years ago.

In addition, Heidi has a debit card for her bank account. Since she is over eighteen years of age, her account is no longer a custodial account but part of her trust with both of our names on the checks. Because she is not able to manage her own account, she is not allowed to have her own debit card; however, we have worked around that. My name is on the card to her account, and I let her carry it with her all the time. That sounds a little dangerous, doesn't it? Well, she actually takes very good care of that card and has never lost it, which is saying more than her mother can say for herself. There has only been one, funny thing she has done with the card, and it truly amazed me. One day when I was balancing her checking account, I noticed a $1.50 expense and realized she had bought a pop when she didn't have any cash. Wow, quite a girl I say—especially since I never showed her how to use the card in a pop machine! Heidi's pop intake is restricted because it adds to her weight problem, so maybe she was mad with no money and figured out how she could have her way.

Another Christmas came, and again I asked her what she wanted. She responded, "A musical clock." I didn't buy it right away, but then I realized her alarm clock was rather annoying when it woke her up in the morning. In response, I went to Target and bought her a large radio/alarm/CD clock. Unfortunately, it has been a real challenge for many of us to figure out how to play the thing. It has a teeny-tiny remote control (less than half the size of your palm) from which all information is communicated to the clock. It took almost a year until we finally managed to get that thing running, but we did it. Now when I go into her room, she is lying there and listening to relaxing Christian piano music from a CD a friend gave to us. It makes me smile, and I agree that she has the right idea about how to wake up in the best way possible.

Heidi's latest toy is her new IPad. While she still has an old one, the newer one has so much more, and she discovers all kinds of things on it. Her little sister has also set up the IPad with the proper safeguards. I believe and have told Heidi that, in some ways, she is smarter than I am. She just doesn't want us to know how smart she is.

···55···
Down in the Pit

ONCE AGAIN, I was in need of prayer from my friends. I just couldn't get out of the pit of depression, so they brought to mind Psalm 42, which speaks about being brought out of a pit. Serving a special needs child takes relinquishing my rights many times for many years. Anyone who takes care of a seriously ill person must do the same thing, and the relinquishing might even have to be done on a daily basis. Thus, my friends prayed for me and brought me up out of my pit of despair. I was relieved and free again to serve Heidi with love and grace.

Since this last prayer time, I had another talk with God. I was on my way to some friends' home out-of-town, and while driving I said to the Lord, "I accept Heidi into my life. You said You'd give me grace for every step, and I accept it." Then I heard the following words: "Heidi will not prevent you from doing anything you are supposed to do. She might even help you!" Ouch! Nailed again by the truth of God's word.

Her Name Is Heidi

There have been many times when I have either just put her to bed or watched her sleep that I've asked God, "Just who is she?" While I don't always get an answer, the latest time I asked, He responded, "It's Me." I thought, "It's Me?" What a surprise! But is it really a surprise? How we treat others, especially children, is really how we treat Him.

This is good for me. I receive her, again.

···56···
Heidi's Neighbor

WHEN HEIDI WAS just one, we moved into a large brick home with four bedrooms, two full baths, and a nice yard. It also had a huge living room that fit two pianos and a large dining room as well. We moved there in the middle of the winter, so we didn't meet our neighbor until early one spring day. I met her over the backyard fence, and we hit it off right away.

Heidi hit it off with her as well. It seems that wherever we lived, there was a willing lady next-door or close by who liked to help with my children. It was good for the kids, good for me, and good for the ladies who had so much love in their hearts that they just had to share it with our children.

This particular neighbor was Thelma, and she was about 68 years old when we first met. Eventually, we did almost everything together. I gave her iced tea when she mowed her yard, and she gave me iced coffee when I mowed mine. She would come over to visit and join in on whatever activity was happening at the moment. When summer came, our family set up a picnic table on the back porch and put a

Her Name Is Heidi

board over the stairs. Heidi loved being outside, yet protected by her backdoor playpen, and she would look over the board, see folks coming, and laugh and smile. Thelma was one of her favorites.

Thelma was also there when Heidi had her open-heart surgery at twenty-two months old and weighing only sixteen pounds. When Heidi became stronger, she would raise her little arms to Thelma as soon as she entered the kitchen and off they went! Thelma would hold her little hands, and they would walk together into the living room and up the stairs. Wherever Heidi wanted to go, that's where they went. I don't know how Thelma did it, but she loved her. As my two girls grew older, they would go into Thelma's backyard and play there. Thelma would get out her jump rope and show them how to do it. What an amazing woman!

After we moved into an apartment, I had to leave for work before Heidi even woke up to go to middle school. Still, Heidi woke up, got dressed, and walked down the hall to Thelma's apartment all by herself. When she arrived, Thelma had her breakfast ready on a tray and brought it to the chair where Heidi was sitting. One time I came in, and Heidi looked like a princess. I realized then that Heidi had

Thelma wrapped around her little finger. After breakfast, Thelma would walk Heidi down the hall where they could see the school bus arrive. They were two peas in a pod, and I was so grateful for all the help.

If we went to a metro park, Thelma came along and pushed the girls on the swings. One time she did "under doggie" and ever so gracefully (and in slow motion) fell into the mulch. She was not hurt, and boy did we laugh. It wasn't until years later that I finally realized how close Thelma was to Heidi. We were going through a photo album, and she looked at a picture of Heidi and said, "That's my girl!"

Now at 104 years of age, Thelma is still here, and we visit her at the assisted living home. Thelma still gets a kick out of Heidi when she says funny things and eats with real gusto. Heidi puts a smile on Thelma's face, which makes the visit worthwhile, and for some reason Heidi still calls Thelma, "my neighbor."

...57...
Being a Care Provider

WHERE I LIVE in Columbus, Ohio there is a job known as a Parent Directed Provider (PDP). I tried to get into the system five years ago, but the paperwork was sidetracked so it didn't happen. However, this time it did.

For those of you who are parents of a child with an Individual Education Plan (IEP) during their school years or a child with an Individual Service Plan (ISP) for their adult years, you might be able to take advantage of this parent program (PDP). Why would you want to do this? I have found that even though Heidi has providers to take her out after work and on Saturdays, the organizations are all understaffed, but I am not sure why. Maybe the requirements are set high? Regardless, Heidi progressed from a Level 1 Waiver and is now on an IO Waiver. I don't quite understand how the waivers all work, but I do know that it is about funding and my turning 65. And while we have all kinds of money available to serve Heidi, there is no one to do it.

One night I woke up with the thought of trying again to be her parent provider because it involves doing all the things I am already doing with Heidi, which are in her ISP goals. The only difference is that I will get paid for it. If you want to do this, first and foremost, contact your child's case manager. The manager has to be a part of this, plus you'll need the help and guidance. Managers will tell you how to start the process, whom to contact, and how to do it, and they also have to submit the ISP to the organization. It is less expensive to pay parents to take care of their adult children at home than having the children live in a group home.

So, after talking to Heidi's caseworker, I filled out some paperwork, went in to the hiring interview, and had my fingerprints taken. Once accepted, I took waiver training, CPR, and first aid, and I decided to be hired under one of the companies that already serves Heidi. If I became an independent provider, it would involve all kinds of tax and income paperwork, which I don't want to do.

I am only finishing my third week as a parent provider, but it has been quite amazing. The first week, Heidi didn't have providers at all, which can happen sometimes, so I explained to her, as I whisked her off to the YMCA right after work, that I was her provider for the day. We walked, then came home, and fixed dinner together, including clean up. It was amazing to see how much time I did work with her. Her service coordinator told me that once I kept track of how much I did with Heidi, I would be surprised by how much time I actually put into her care, and I have, in fact, been surprised.

Hopefully I will be able to keep up with Heidi on the long walks and other activities. Doing housework, kitchen clean up, and laundry can be tiring, but so far, I am doing it. Now I have an extra income without having to go out in the "world," and it's quite a blessing for which I am grateful and both of us are enjoying.

Now during this pandemic virus of 2020, Heidi has no providers, so it is wonderful timing for us to increase our time and work together. Yesterday we walked in a new park and put in a mile or so. We also climbed on some playground equipment that was new and exciting for Heidi. At another park we came across one of those "little library" boxes! Since we can't go to the libraries yet, it was so fun to get some new books. She was excited and jumping, laughing, and giggling about her new books. It was a special day. While I must admit that I had to take some ibuprofen when I arrived home, I kept up with her all the way, and she seems to think that going out with Mom isn't so bad after all.

···58···
In Her Own Words

IT'S ME, HEIDI. I am 37 and can't wait until my birthday in eight months. I like to go out, like everybody else my age. I like to pick what I want to do, what I eat, and what I drink. I like to wear shorts, and I love my IPad.

When Mom read a part of this story to me, it made me laugh. I remembered what she was talking about. I want her to read more of it to me. I like being home more now since my workshop closed because of the virus. I sleep until noon every day then Mom or Andrew does things with me at home and we go out too.

Mom takes me out every day to walk. We go to parks where there aren't many people. Mom likes the parks that have water. Andrew takes me out to deliver Uber Eats meals. I love going with him. He makes it so much fun. He lets me put some of the meals on the front porches and pays me for my work. I love getting paid, and I love being with my brother. Sometimes he does little dances while delivering, and it makes me laugh.

Her Name Is Heidi

When people ask me questions, sometimes I don't know what to say. If I fall or am sad or cry, they ask me, "What happened?" It's too hard to explain, so I don't say anything. Sometimes this makes them upset or angry.

I don't like it when my mom goes to New York by herself to see Granny. But Mom says that she has to have time with her mom too. I don't like dark rooms or storms either. Mom lights candles around me and then I am not so afraid.

One of my favorite TV shows is *Keeping Up Appearances*. I laugh even before a funny part comes because I know what they are going to say. I like the *Pink Panther* movies too. I say a lot of their expressions and laugh all over again.

Mom has been teaching me how to put pills in my pillboxes. I didn't like learning it, but now that I am getting better at it, I don't mind doing it by myself. After dinner, I usually tell Mom that it was a lovely meal. I also tell her, "Thank you for all you do for me." She smiles and says, "You're welcome, and thank you for all you do for me too!"

...59...
To Heidi

To Heidi I write this,
To the answer of many prayers.
For the gentle and quiet spirit within,
To live in faith and not despair.

Through you, my child, I see His face,
His love and peace within.
Lord, make me simple as my child,
Not bound up and restricted in sin.

For you, I praise the Father,
For the testing and the fire.
I cannot escape as I did in past,
But a higher level I must acquire.

Her Name Is Heidi

To walk with you, my little one,
To hold you by the hand,
To be your helper and faithful coach,
To lead you to His land.

To walk with you is a privilege,
An honor before God, it's true.
I don't deserve you or His love.
Lord, make me more like You.

The future is in His Hands, dear one,
For you and me and Dad.
As long as we seek His precious will
And do it, we'll be glad.

So I write this book about you,
For I know you are sent from God.
Now may it bless some other soul
And help them walk this sod.

Acknowledgements

I want to thank Allison Myers, my editor, who made the rough places plain. I also want to thank my fellow comrades, who picked me up when I fainted, stumbled, and fell. Their years of faithful support made this story possible.